CW00498674

# PIZZA & SAVOURY BREADS COOKBOOK

Joanne Glynn

PHOTOGRAPHY BY QUENTIN BACON
STYLING BY DONNA HAY

BayBooks
An imprint of HarperCollins*Publishers*

STOCKIST

Appley Hoare Antiques
55 Queen Street
Woollahra NSW 2025
Tel: (02) 362 3045

A BAY BOOKS PUBLICATION

Bay Books, an imprint of
HarperCollinsPublishers
25 Ryde Road Pymble, Sydney NSW 2073, Australia
31 View Road, Glenfield, Auckland 10, New Zealand

First published in Australia in 1994



National Library of Australia
Cataloguing-in-Publication data:

Glynn, Joanne.
Pizza and savoury breads.
Includes index.
ISBN 1 86378 173 0.
1. Pizza. 2.Bread. I. Title.
641.815

Photographer: Quentin Bacon
Food Stylist: Donna Hay
Home Economist: Jody Vassallo
Food Stylist's Assistant: Darienne Sutton

Front Cover Recipes: Scallop, Zucchini (Courgette) and Basil Pizza; Potato Bread with Bacon and Onion; Onion and Black Pepper Grissini; Spinach and Cheese Puffs; Mini Panzarotti with Gorgonzola and Walnuts
Printed in Australia by Griffin Press, Adelaide

5 4 3 2 1
97 96 95 94

# CONTENTS

~

# Introduction

Bread is the staff of life, so the saying goes, and its presence is so well entrenched in history that it has become fundamental to our everyday needs and pleasures.

It is known that Neolithic man gathered wild grain, ground it and mixed it with water. This was boiled into a kind of porridge or gruel and was the forerunner to bread.

Stone Age farmers first cultivated barley and wheat in the fertile lands sweeping from the Nile up to the area now known as Iran. This ensured variety and the availability of their grain. They cooked the mushy porridge by spreading it thinly onto heated flat stones, much the same way as we make pancakes or pikelets today. This was the first flatbread. By the Bronze Age, 5000 years ago, a primitive oven was being used by inverting pots over hot cooking stones to capture the heat.

The ancient Egyptians constructed the first fixed ovens and it was also these wise and inventive people who learnt the mysteries of yeast fermentation. It had been known that dough that was left out in the open for a number of hours would often bubble and smell sour, and if this was baked the resulting bread was lighter and had a pleasing flavour. This natural fermentation was caused by airborne yeast but it was pretty much a hit and miss affair and could not be relied on to produce a standard and controllable reaction.

What the Egyptians did was to simply save a piece of fermented dough from a previously successful leavening and mix it in with the new dough. This practice is still common today.

All around the Mediterranean the different civilisations developed bread making. As people fanned out into the territories and kingdoms of others, a natural adoption of their particular baking skills by the indigenous people often occurred. In particular the influence of the ancient Greeks was pronounced, as they literally worshipped bread and baking was an integral part of their culture.

This reverence was passed on to the Romans. It is said that the habit of marking a cross on the surface of pre-baked bread to aid rising probably arose from the Roman Christian tradition of making the sign of the cross over dough before baking and then over the bread before breaking.

Once the basic loaf became commonplace it was improved upon by adding other ingredients; probably little more than a smattering of herbs and oil initially. In the days when salt was beyond the purse of the man in the street, anchovies were a favourite flavouring, while the ancient Mesopotamians used fruits and honey instead of sugar. Adventurous bakers began incorporating more substantial ingredients: olives, wild mushrooms, clams and sardines, whatever was grown or gathered locally, giving the bread more content and producing a transportable and nutritious meal all in one golden package!

Flatbreads and hearthbreads were country breads baked on the hearths of farmhouses. Being a less sophisticated form of baking, they have always been important and have remained pretty much unchanged. Today in Spain's Balearic Islands one can find the coca de Baleares, in France they have the pissaladiere and Italy has the pizza, all remarkably similar. Piadina, small discs of unleavened dough used to fold around a filling in some parts of Italy, are a close relative of both the Spanish empanada and the flat Arab breads used to wrap around food. These similarities occur time and again right around the Mediterranean, Europe and the Middle East, and of course as populations expanded and settled further afield, along went their breads.

Look at the pizza which started

humbly as street food for the poor in Naples. A simple form of flatbread had been enjoyed there from as early as the time of the ancient Greek occupation. By the middle of the 18th century the average Neapolitan, not having an oven at home, was buying hot slices of dough baked with oil and perhaps some herbs, from roaming street vendors. The more up-market pizza seller operated out of a kiosk and offered toppings such as anchovies, mushrooms or cheese. This practice progressed into the pizzaioli who baked his wares in a small, fixed stand, and then, sometime around 1830, the first pizzeria was opened. It was a place where customers could sit down and wile away the hours over a pizza baked to order and a glass or two of wine. It wasn't really until after the Second World War, when the Neapolitans left Naples in search of work in the more prosperous north and took their favourite food with them, that pizzerias became popular elsewhere in Italy. Wherever the Neapolitan migrated to and settled, there too went the pizza and it very quickly became universally beloved.

No matter where the meal or what the occasion, savoury breads have remained a simple but very satisfying staple with endless variations. They have stayed in the repertoire of the home cook and in fact, with modern technology and more widely available ingredients, they are easier than ever before to bake at home.

# Bread Basics

Bread making is simplicity itself, but too often cooks are daunted by the many rules and lengthy explanations. By giving it a go a couple of times, all those instructions will fall into place and become second nature in no time! The actual 'hands on' time is not long, and the separate steps can be slotted in between other household demands. Unlike the more conventional plain bread loaves, where misjudgment or inexperience can give a bad result, the addition of other ingredients in savoury breads camouflages an imperfect dough.

**Ingredients**

**Flour** There is now a great variety of flour blends and styles available to the home baker, from low gluten cake flour to high gluten bread flour. The latter is designed for bakers with commercial machinery hardy enough to cope with the strong and long kneading necessary and ovens able to maintain very high temperatures.

Bread flour is generally not recommended for the home baker who will be kneading by hand or at best in a domestic mixer, and baking in a domestic oven.

Plain flour, also called baker's or all-purpose flour, is ideal for our needs where supporting height and volume is not a priority.

Sometimes a specially blended pizza flour is available that is also good to use in most savoury loaves as well as in flatbreads. Unbleached flour will give your dough a subtly different flavour and texture as well as extra vitamin B.

Wholemeal or wholewheat flour is milled, as the name suggests, from the entire wheat grain, not just the endosperm as with white flour. It contains more vitamins, oils and dietary fibre but less gluten, and therefore, makes a heavier loaf. It is darker in colour and gives a nutty flavour and coarser texture to bread.

Other grains apart from wheat can be used and it's one of the joys of home baking that you can experiment with these to achieve different flavours and textures. Bear in mind, though, that most other bread grains have little or no gluten and should be blended with wheat flour when using yeast. Cornmeal, rye flour, buckwheat, oatmeal and barley flour all fall into this category. A proportion of one of these in your dough gives alternative nutritional value as well as interest.

Semolina is a particular grind of wheat flour. It is a coarse, recognisable meal as opposed to the powder texture of regular flour. Durum wheat semolina, for instance, is made from the hard durum wheat and a proportion of this in bread dough gives a golden tinge and a delicious, slightly nutty flavour. Semolina from ordinary wheat will still give an interesting texture.

**Yeast and Leavening Agents** Leavens in dough release gas, causing it to expand and rise.

As well as texture and volume in the final loaf, the flour used and the resulting flavour are considerations when determining the choice of leaven. For our recipes, bicarbonate of soda, baking powder and yeast are used; all are readily available these days.

Bicarbonate of soda is a common leaven in savoury bread baking. When it comes into contact with water and then heat it gives off carbon dioxide which aerates the dough, thus raising and supporting the loaf. However, it has an alkaline, soapy taste and needs to be neutralised by an acid. When it is combined with cream of tartar, not only is the flavour adjusted but a reaction occurs that further encourages the production of gas. This combination, plus a little cornflour to keep it dry, is what we know as baking powder. When only bicarbonate of soda is used, soured milk or buttermilk is needed to neutralise the taste.

The obvious benefit of using non-yeast raising agents is time saving, as little, if any kneading is necessary and no time is required for *proving*. (This term is applied to the final rising process. This process is necessary so that the activating yeast can lift and then uphold the dough at double its original size. The time involved can be anywhere between 30 minutes and 1½ hours.) Unyeasted breads don't keep as long, their texture is coarser and the loaf is not as light.

Yeast is available in two main

forms: blocks of compressed fresh yeast, and little sealed sachets of granulated dried yeast. Compressed fresh yeast is the colour of putty, feels a bit like modelling clay and has a fresh, slightly alcoholic smell. If kept chilled in an airtight container it has a life of approximately one week before it deteriorates.

Granulated or active dry yeast is more readily available and has a shelf life of approximately twelve months. The contents of each sachet, whatever the brand, are always 7 g (¼ oz) as this is the accepted amount used with 3 cups (375 g/12 oz) of flour for an average-sized loaf. If you want to use less than 1 sachet (for instance, to halve a recipe) the remaining half sachet must be discarded as, once opened, it begins to spoil immediately and becomes useless. An economical way around this is to make the full recipe, bake half and freeze the remainder. Many makers today have developed their product so that it can be mixed directly with the dry ingredients, thus cutting out the need to activate the yeast with warm water. To be safe, our recipes all go through this 5 minute step regardless; it can't hurt and it is a sure way of testing the viability of your yeast before proceeding too far. If it doesn't activate with the warm water and start to foam after 5 minutes it is stale, so discard it and start again with a fresh sachet.

In all our recipes using yeast, active dry yeast is called for, however, fresh and dried yeast are interchangeable, if you remember two points: use twice as much by weight of fresh yeast as dried; and the temperatures needed to activate the yeasts differ — 37°C to 38°C (99°F to 100°F) for fresh and 41°C to 43°C (106°F to 109°F) for dried.

Apart from starting with active yeast, the other important thing is temperature. Too much heat and it will kill the yeast, too little initially and there's not enough to activate fermentation. Once the dough has been kneaded, however, low temperatures are preferred; long, cool rising, ideally at around 22°C (72°F) gives a better flavoured bread.

A yeast compound in powdered form is now available. Designed for bread making with hard flours and for mixing directly with the flour, it is too powerful for our purposes and not recommended.

**Liquids** For most breads water is traditionally the liquid used. However, by substituting a proportion of milk a smoother dough with a richer colour and flavour results and is sometimes preferred.

Olive oil can be incorporated into the dough of pizza or flatbreads and here again the texture and flavour is improved.

For home baking, olive oil makes the dough easier to knead by hand and it responds better to a domestic oven. Extra virgin olive oil is preferred for its flavour and low acidity.

In recipes using eggs, have them at room temperature and beat lightly together before use.

**Salt** Salt restricts the activity of yeast and so should never be added directly to it. Either blend it through the flour before liquids are added or wait until the final stages of mixing the dough and blend it in then.

Savoury breads will take on a lot of flavour from the additional ingredients used. With this in mind, the salt used in their doughs should be just enough to stimulate the gluten in the flour and bring out its inherent nutty flavour.

## Equipment

The best aids to home bread baking are a big flat even surface, a big heavy bowl and a reliable oven that can maintain high temperatures.

There are many other pieces of equipment that make your work easier and perhaps quicker, but they aren't a necessity.

Firstly, a heavy-duty benchtop electric mixer with a well designed dough hook takes the heavy work out of kneading doughs. Food processors are fine for blending and mixing ingredients, but for kneading yeast doughs, the high heat generated requires a specific method using cold liquids, and a final hand kneading is required anyway.

Another consideration is appropriate tins for the various shapes and sizes of bread. For deep-sided loaves, blackened heavy gauge steel or tin will retain heat more than shiny metal and give a crisp crust. For unmoulded loaves use a porous baking stone as described below for pizza, or a flat oven tray made of non-stick heavy-duty steel or aluminium. This is also ideal for baking small flatbreads, bread sticks and rolls. When baking calzone or flatbreads with a topping, which may leak, use a non-stick heavy-duty baking tray with a slight rim to catch any spillage.

A good rolling pin is a definite advantage. The most efficient one is about 50 cm (20 in) long and tapers off towards the ends.

Other implements that come in handy are a dough scraper, a little whisk for whipping smooth the activated yeast before blending it with flour, a cooling rack and, if you're nervous about judging temperatures, an instant reading thermometer.

**Particularly for Pizza**

In order to form a crisp crust, pizzas need to bake on a flat, porous surface that absorbs moisture but conducts intense heat evenly and quickly. What best replicates the floor of a pizza oven is a porous baking stone, available in different sizes from specialty kitchen shops. Roughly the same effect can be achieved by positioning a number of unglazed quarry tiles together on the oven rack, but the drawback with this is that if they're knocked and part from each other, the gaps cause uneven heating and can be messy when you have the inevitable leak of topping or oil. With this system, the stone or tiles are pre-heated along with the oven and so the pizza must be transported from the kitchen bench to the stone. For this job there are two utensils available for pizza aficionados. The first is a pizza peel or paddle which is a flat wooden board with a long handle, as seen in your local pizzeria. The other is a pizza screen, a circle of heavy gauge metal mesh with a strong metal rim. However, it is quite acceptable to simply compile the pizza on a tray or plate and slip it onto the tiles in the oven.

There is a pizza tray available that is made from a double thickness of aluminium and has hundreds of holes evenly distributed over its centre. As aluminium is a great conductor of heat, this is a very good alternative: moisture can escape, giving a crisp crust, it is strong, and it doesn't rust. However, if none of the above are obtainable, a blackened steel or non-stick oven tray or round pizza tray strong enough to prevent buckling all work well.

Ever wondered what those dinky little olive oil cans are for? They're great for drizzling oil over the pizza and a pastry brush comes in handy for oiling the pastry rim.

A pizza wheel cuts cooked pizza without dragging the topping off, and for serving the slices, a strong and long metal spatula is ideal.

# PIZZA

The pizza began as simply garnished flatbread sold by roaming vendors to the poor in the streets of 18th century Naples. Probably the biggest step towards its present-day persona was the acceptance of the tomato by the Neapolitans, and the subsequent use of its flesh as a pizza topping.

This happy culinary partnership was endorsed, so the story goes, in 1889 when Queen Margherita was accompanying her husband, Umberto I of Savoia on an inspection of his Italian kingdom. She was extremely popular with the masses and had developed a great liking for their pizza. This taste was considered somewhat undesirable in court circles, so one day in June, Raffaele Esposito was summoned from his pizzeria to the palace to bake a selection of pizza for the queen. When news got out that her favourite was topped with tomato, mozzarella and basil (the colours of the Italian flag), she not only became an even greater hit with the public, but started a trend for the pizza Margherita that has lasted in Naples to this day.

Not all so-called pizza are flat; calzone and panzarotti, for example, are filled turnovers. Originally from Apulia, they became popular in Naples where simple turnovers were being made with scraps of pizza dough. Their making went hand in hand with pizza making and so they came to be thought of in the same vein. The names we know them by, in fact, are old Naples dialect. You will find recipes for these and other stuffed breads in the Filled Breads chapter.

*Thick Pizza with Sun-dried Tomato Paste, Artichokes and Parmesan (page 30); Green Asparagus and Parmesan Pizzette with Cornmeal Dough (page 30)*

**≈ Pizza Dough**

*Each of the recipes below includes a recommended pizza dough, but these are suggestions only. You can interchange doughs, shapes or sizes as it's all part of the fun of pizza. Using shop bought bases is quite acceptable; just bear in mind that the oven temperatures required may differ so check the maker's instructions. It is also recommended to lightly dampen a pre-baked base. This will create moisture in the oven and give a crisp, as opposed to a dry, crust and it freshens the dough.*

*Only one rising is needed with yeast doughs before they are ready to shape into the desired pizza base. If the dough is not to be used within 2 to 3 hours of this rising, punch it down, coat with oil again and return to the bowl. Seal tightly with plastic and refrigerate. It can now rise slowly over 8 to 10 hours, until doubled in bulk. This step can be repeated three times without the dough spoiling. Alternatively, the dough may be frozen after the first rising and left for up to 3 months. Just defrost and bring to room temperature before proceeding.*

# Base Recipes

## BASIC PIZZA DOUGH

**3 teaspoons caster sugar**

**85 ml (3 fl oz) warm water (41°C to 42°C/106°F to 108°F, comfortable to the fingers)**

**1 sachet (7 g/¼ oz) active dry yeast**

**435 g (14 oz) plain (baker's/all-purpose) flour**

**½ teaspoon salt**

**65 ml (2 fl oz) olive oil**

**125 ml (4 fl oz) warm water, extra, temperature as above**

**1** In a cup or small bowl blend sugar and the 85 ml (3 fl oz) warm water. Add yeast, gently stir to combine then set aside in a protected spot. Within 5 minutes the mixture will activate and foam, forming the sponge. If no bubbling occurs, discard and start again with a fresh sachet of yeast.

**2** Combine flour and salt in a large bowl. Add olive oil, the sponge and 125 ml (4 fl oz) of warm water. Using a wooden spoon mix liquids with dry ingredients until dough holds together and clumps around the spoon.

**3** Transfer to a lightly floured surface and knead into a ball. The dough should be soft, but dry to the heel of your hands. If it is necessary to correct the balance, knead in flour or warm water sparingly. A dough which is too dry gives dry, heavy bread.

**4** Knead dough until it is smooth and elastic; at least 12 minutes. Don't cheat on the timing; it is necessary to develop the gluten. The dough is sufficiently kneaded when a firm finger imprint springs back out leaving little or no impression. This step may be done in a heavy-duty electric mixer with a dough hook attachment, following the manufacturer's instructions.

**5** Transfer dough to a large bowl which has been well oiled. Roll dough around several times to coat. This will prevent a hard crust forming on the surface, which can inhibit rising. With a small knife cut a shallow cross on the top. Seal bowl tightly with cling wrap. If this doesn't cling to the bowl successfully, use a large plastic bag and wrap the bowl up well, tucking the opening under the bowl to create the humid atmosphere necessary for the yeast to develop.

**6** Place bowl in a protected spot, free from draughts or direct sunlight. The cooler the environment, the longer the rising but the lighter the bread. The dough needs to double in volume, usually after 1 to 1½ hours at normal room temperature.

**7** Remove dough from bowl and punch down to its original size. It is now ready to be divided and shaped. If using a rolling pin, roll out on a lightly floured surface to three quarters of the desired size, then do the final shaping by hand. Beginning in the centre and working out, evenly flatten dough with the heel of the hand. Lighten the pressure 1 to 2 cm (½ to ¾ in) from the edge to create a slightly raised rim. The pizza may be shaped from scratch in this way.

**Makes 1 x 42 cm (17 in), 2 x 30 cm (12 in), or 8 x 17 cm (6¾ in) round pizzas**

## WHOLEMEAL PIZZA DOUGH

**3 teaspoons caster sugar or honey**

**85 ml (3 fl oz) warm water (41°C to 42°C/106°F to 108°F, comfortable to the fingers)**

**1 sachet (7 g/¼ oz) active dry yeast**

**155 g (5 oz) plain (baker's/all-purpose) flour**

**310 g (10 oz) wholemeal flour**

**½ teaspoon salt**

**65 ml (2 fl oz) olive oil**

**190 ml (6 fl oz) warm water, temperature as above**

Follow method for Basic Pizza Dough (see recipe page 10), adding wholemeal flour to the plain flour and salt.

## YEASTLESS PIZZA DOUGH

**375 g (12 oz) plain (baker's/all-purpose) flour**

**½ teaspoon baking powder**

**1½ tablespoons caster sugar**

**½ teaspoon salt**

**2 eggs, lightly beaten**

**150 ml (5 fl oz) olive oil**

**80 ml (2½ fl oz) dry white wine**

**1** This step may be done in a food processor. Combine flour, baking powder, sugar and salt in a bowl. Using a wooden spoon, gradually mix in eggs, oil and wine. When mixture is loosely combined and clumps around the spoon, transfer to a floured surface.

**2** Finish mixing by hand, then knead for 3 to 4 minutes until smooth and glossy. Cover and rest at room temperature for at least 30 minutes before use. Alternatively, cover well with plastic wrap or a plastic bag and store in the refrigerator until ready for use; up to 5 days. Bring to room temperature, knead lightly to incorporate any oil which may have separated then roll out to desired thickness.

**MAKES 1 X 38 CM (15 IN), 2 X 26 CM (10½ IN) ROUND PIZZAS OR ONE 36 CM X 40 CM (14½ X 16 IN) RECTANGULAR PIZZA**

## YEASTLESS WHOLEMEAL PIZZA DOUGH

**185 g (6 oz) plain (baker's/all-purpose) flour**

**235 g (7½ oz) wholemeal flour**

**¾ teaspoon baking powder**

**1½ tablespoons caster sugar**

**½ teaspoon salt**

**2 eggs, lightly beaten**

**150 ml (5 fl oz) olive oil**

**100 ml (3½ fl oz) dry white wine**

Follow method for Yeastless Pizza Dough (see recipe this page), adding the wholemeal flour to the dry ingredients.

**≈ YEASTLESS PIZZA DOUGH**

*This dough is ideal for those who prefer a thin crust. It is easy to handle and the combination of sugar, white wine and olive oil gives a subtle fermented flavour.*
*If replacing a yeast dough with this one, roll it 5 mm (¼ in) thicker than specified as it won't rise as much. Bake at 220°C (425°F) and allow an extra 5 minutes baking time.*

*Pizza Dough*

**≈ Baked Eggplant (Aubergine), Bocconcini and Red Capsicum (Pepper) Pizza**

*The interesting combination of flavours here uses eggplant (aubergine) pulp as the base sauce. Its slightly nutty taste nicely complements wholemeal dough, but other bases work well too. Choose two or three young, small eggplant (aubergine) as these usually have a high flesh to seed ratio.*

# BAKED EGGPLANT (AUBERGINE), BOCCONCINI AND RED CAPSICUM (PEPPER) PIZZA

**1 x recipe Wholemeal Pizza Dough, (see recipe page 10)**

**3 to 4 eggplant (aubergine) (totalling 1.5 kg/3 lb)**

**3 garlic cloves, cut into slivers**

**salt and freshly ground black pepper**

**1 large red capsicum (pepper), cut into strips 2 to 3 cm (¾ in to 1¼ in) long**

**200 g (6½ oz) bocconcini or fresh mozzarella cheese, cut into 1 cm (½ in) cubes**

**1 tablespoon chopped chives (optional)**

**3 tablespoons olive oil**

**1** Preheat oven to 200°C (400°F) and lightly oil two 32 cm (12¾ in) diameter pizza trays.

**2** Divide dough in two, then roll out and shape each on a floured surface to a circle approximately 30 cm (12 in) diameter with a slightly raised rim. Transfer to prepared trays and cover with tea towels.

**3** Pierce each eggplant (aubergine) 6 to 8 times evenly over its body, and insert a sliver of garlic into the slits. Place directly onto oven racks, untouching. Bake for 50 to 60 minutes, or until the skins are wrinkled and the flesh, when prodded, feels soft and sloppy. Remove from oven and raise the temperature to 230°C (450°F). When eggplant (aubergine) are cool enough to handle, cut open and discard seeds and skin. Transfer the pulp, including garlic, to a bowl. Mash with a fork until coarsely smooth, then add salt and pepper to taste.

**4** Spread eggplant (aubergine) paste evenly over each dough base. Distribute bocconcini, capsicum (pepper) strips and chives over surface. Drizzle olive oil over the top.

**5** Transfer to oven and bake until golden, 15 to 18 minutes.

**Makes two 30 cm to 32 cm (12 in to 12¾ in) pizzas**

# BLUE CHEESE AND SAGE PIZZA

*This pizza is just as good served cold, cut into fingers as it is straight from the oven.*

**1 x recipe Basic Pizza Dough, (see recipe page 10)**

**300 g (10 oz) soft blue vein cheese, such as gorgonzola or Blue Castello**

**300 g (10 oz) grated mozzarella cheese**

**a few fresh sage leaves, torn or chopped into small pieces**

**1** Preheat oven to 220°C (425°F) and brush a large rectangular baking tray with oil.

**2** Roll out or shape dough on a floured surface to a rectangle roughly 30 cm x 45 cm (12 in x 18 in). Transfer to prepared tray.

**3** Mash blue cheese in a bowl, then stir in mozzarella.

**4** Spread cheese mixture evenly over the surface, going to within 1 cm (½ in) of the edge, then sprinkle sage over the top.

**5** Transfer to the oven and bake until dough is golden and the cheeses bubbling, about 12 minutes.

**6** Cool for a minute or two before serving, or cool completely and serve cold.

**Makes 1 pizza 30 cm x 45 cm (12 in x 18 in)**

*Blue Cheese and Sage Pizza; Baked Eggplant (Aubergine), Bocconcini and Red Capsicum (Pepper) Pizza*

≈ **Potato, Rosemary and Cheese Pizzette**

*Don't be deceived by the simplicity of the ingredients here. These little pizzas look very elegant and the taste is subtle.*

# POTATO, ROSEMARY AND CHEESE PIZZETTE

**1 x recipe Basic Pizza Dough, (see recipe page 10)**

**3 large (approximately 1 kg/2 lb) potatoes**

**250 g (8 oz) grated tasty cheddar cheese**

**a 6 cm (2½ in) sprig fresh rosemary**

**extra virgin olive oil**

**1** Preheat oven to 250°C (475°F) and lightly flour 2 heavy-duty baking trays.

**2** Divide dough into 8. Roll out each piece on a floured surface into a disc approximately 15 cm (6 in) diameter, then by hand stretch out to roughly 17 cm (6¾ in) with a slightly raised rim. Position on baking trays.

**3** Peel potatoes and slice very thinly.

**4** Sprinkle grated cheese over each base, then arrange potato slices, slightly

overlapping, over the top. Sprinkle rosemary leaves on the top.

**5** Brush the pastry rim with a little olive oil then drizzle a little more over the potatoes.

**6** Transfer to oven and bake until dough is crisp and potatoes golden, 10 to 15 minutes. If they appear to be baking unevenly, swap tray positions after 8 minutes.

**MAKES 8 X PIZZETTE OF APPROXIMATELY 17 CM (6¾ IN) DIAMETER**

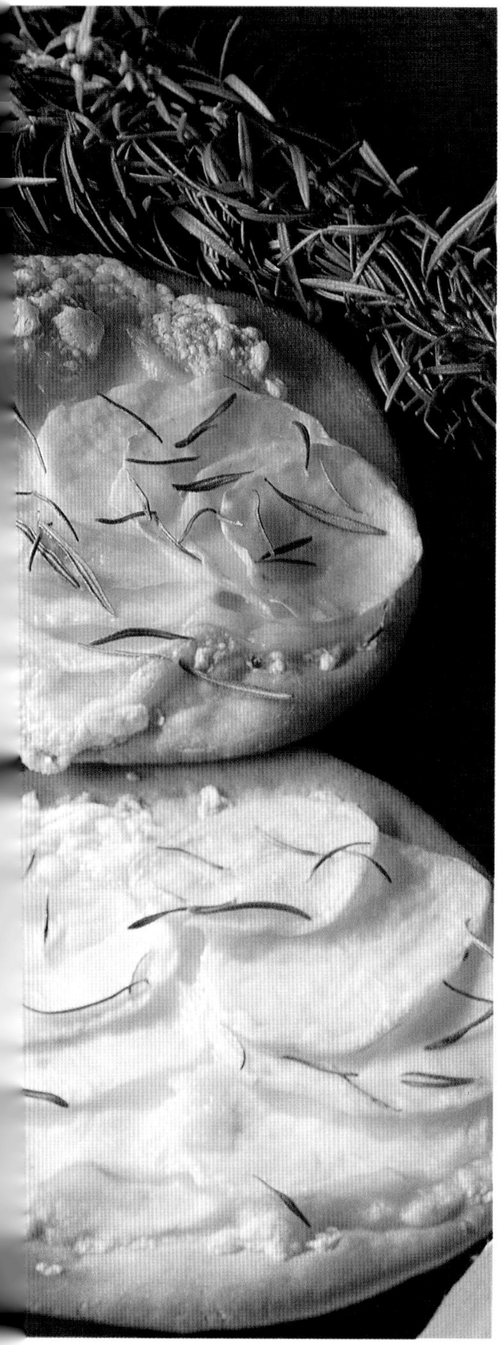

Potato, Rosemary and Cheese Pizzette

# CLAM BAKE

**1 x recipe Wholemeal Pizza Dough, (see recipe page 10)**

**extra virgin olive oil**

**500 g (16 oz) shredded cheddar cheese**

**750 g (24 oz) drained cooked clams without shells**

**3 large tomatoes, skinned, seeded and chopped**

**3 garlic cloves, minced**

**salt and freshly ground black pepper**

**3 tablespoons chopped parsley**

**2 pinches chilli flakes**

**1** Preheat oven to 230°C (450°F) and brush two pizza or heavy-duty baking trays with oil.

**2** Divide dough in half and roll or shape each on a floured surface to a 30 cm (12 in) circle and with a slightly raised rim. Transfer to prepared trays and brush with olive oil.

**3** Sprinkle one third of cheddar over each base. Follow this by half the clams then half the tomatoes per pizza. Sprinkle on garlic, salt and pepper, parsley and chilli flakes, then divide remaining one third of cheese between the two. Drizzle olive oil over the surfaces then transfer to oven. Bake until golden, 15 to 20 minutes. If they are baking unevenly, swap shelves after 10 minutes, or you may prefer to bake them separately.

**MAKES TWO 30 CM (12 IN) ROUND PIZZAS**

**≈ CLAM BAKE**

*This topping is ready in minutes when tinned clams are used. If you would prefer to start with fresh clams in the shell you will need 1.5 kg (3 lb). Pop into a large pan of boiling, lightly salted water and cook until most have opened, 3 to 5 minutes. Discard any which have remained closed. Remove clams from shell with a fork but keep 10 to 12 unshelled and use to garnish the pizza before serving.*

**≈ Roman Style Pizza with Mushrooms, Garlic and Oregano**

*When wandering the streets of Rome, it's hard to miss the displays of big, succulent slabs of pizza in the windows of the pizzerias. Individual servings are cut off as ordered and businessmen, school children and tourists alike all queue throughout the day for this most inviting of snacks. Toppings are deceptively simple using few ingredients; in fact, the most popular is Pizza Bianca, with a dressing of just olive oil, salt, garlic and perhaps some rosemary.*

# ROMAN STYLE PIZZA WITH MUSHROOMS, GARLIC AND OREGANO

**½ x recipe Basic Pizza Dough, (see recipe page 10)**

**olive oil, for brushing**

**300 g (10 oz) smoked mozzarella cheese or 150 g (5 oz) mozzarella and 150 g (5 oz) other smoked cheese of your choice, grated**

**200 g (6½ oz) button mushrooms, thinly sliced**

**salt and freshly ground black pepper**

**olive oil, approximately 4 tablespoons**

**3 garlic cloves, minced**

**1 teaspoon finely chopped fresh oregano, or ½ teaspoon dried**

**1** Preheat oven to 220°C (425°F) and brush a heavy-duty baking tray with olive oil.

**2** Roll out and shape dough on a floured surface to a rectangle 20 cm x 38 cm (8 in x 15 in) with a slightly raised rim. Transfer to prepared tray and brush surface with olive oil.

**3** Distribute mozzarella over the top within the rim, then scatter mushrooms over cheese. Salt and pepper to taste. Drizzle olive oil sparingly over mushrooms, moistening all the mushrooms but not creating pools of oil. Sprinkle garlic over the top, followed by the oregano.

**4** Transfer to oven and bake until dough is golden and the cheese bubbling, about 20 minutes.

**Makes 1 rectangular pizza 20 cm x 38 cm (8 in x 15 in)**

# WHOLEMEAL PIZZA WITH LEEKS AND FOUR CHEESES

**1 x recipe Wholemeal Pizza Dough, (see recipe page 10)**

**20 g (½ oz) butter**

**olive oil**

**3 large leeks, white part only, thinly sliced**

**salt and freshly ground black pepper**

**150 g (5 oz) bel paese or other soft creamy cheese, cut into small dice**

**200 g (6½ oz) gorgonzola or other blue vein cheese, crumbled**

**200 g (6½ oz) grated mozzarella cheese**

**100 g (3½ oz) coarsely grated parmesan cheese**

**1 tablespoon finely chopped parsley**

**1** Preheat oven to 220°C (425°F) and brush 2 heavy-duty baking or pizza trays with oil.

**2** Divide dough in half and roll or shape each on a floured surface to a circle of 30 cm (12 in) diameter, a thickness of 5 mm (¼ in) and a slightly raised rim. Transfer to prepared trays and brush surfaces with olive oil.

**3** To make the topping, melt butter and 1 tablespoon of olive oil in a pan and gently sauté leeks until soft. Remove from heat, salt and pepper to taste then drain on absorbent paper.

**4** In a bowl combine the first 3 cheeses. Distribute over the pizza bases, keeping the rims free. Scatter leek rings on top of cheeses, then sprinkle parmesan and parsley on top of these. Drizzle olive oil over the surface.

**5** Transfer to oven and bake until dough is golden and cheeses bubbling, about 15 minutes.

**Makes two 30 cm (12 in) pizzas**

*Roman Style Pizza with Mushrooms, Garlic and Oregano*
*Wholemeal Pizza with Leeks and Four Cheeses*

**≈ Tomato and Black Olive Pizza Pie**

*With a deep crust and a thick, rich topping, this pizza is halfway between a focaccia and a pie in appearance. Unlike most other pizzas it can be eaten cold. Choose fleshy tomatoes with not too much juice; egg or San Marzano tomatoes are ideal if they are in season.*

# TOMATO AND BLACK OLIVE PIZZA PIE

**½ x recipe Yeastless Pizza Dough, (see recipe page 11)**

**4 tablespoons olive oil**

**750 g (24 oz) fresh tomatoes, peeled, seeded and chopped**

**2 garlic cloves, minced**

**¼ teaspoon sugar**

**salt and freshly ground black pepper**

**grated rind of ½ orange**

**1 tablespoon finely chopped parsley**

**½ tablespoon chopped basil**

**100 g (3½ oz) seeded and sliced black olives**

**100 g (3½ oz) fontina or fresh mozzarella cheese, cut into 1 cm (½ in) cubes**

**1 egg, lightly beaten**

**1** Roll out and shape dough to a circle of 22 cm (8¾ in) with a good sized rim around the edge. Transfer to a pizza or baking tray which has been brushed with oil, cover, and set aside.

**2** For the topping, heat olive oil in a large frying pan and gently sauté tomatoes, garlic and sugar for 5 minutes. Salt and pepper to taste and add orange rind. Simmer gently, uncovered, until mixture is thick and tomatoes are completely broken down, a further 20 minutes. Remove from heat and stir in parsley, basil and olives. Cool for 10 minutes, then stir in cheese and egg.

**3** In the meantime preheat oven to 220°C (425°F).

**4** Spread tomato mixture inside rim of pizza base. Transfer to oven and bake until dough is golden, 15 to 20 minutes.

**Makes one 22 cm (8¾ in) pizza**

# SPINACH AND RICOTTA PIZZA

**½ x recipe Wholemeal Pizza Dough, (see recipe page 10)**

**olive oil, for brushing and pouring**

**1.5 kg (3 lb) fresh spinach**

**4 tablespoons olive oil**

**1 tablespoon sultanas, optional**

**2 tablespoons pine nuts**

**3 garlic cloves, minced**

**salt and freshly ground black pepper**

**300 g (10 oz) ricotta cheese**

**100 g (3½ oz) grated fontina or mozzarella cheese**

*Spinach and Ricotta Pizza; Tomato and Black Olive Pizza Pie*

**1** Preheat oven to 220°C (425°F) and brush a baking or pizza tray with olive oil.

**2** Roll out and shape dough on a floured surface to a circle of 28 cm (11 in) diameter with a raised rim, then brush surface with olive oil. Transfer to prepared tray and set aside, loosely covered, until ready to use.

**3** Stem spinach and wash leaves under cold water. Shake off excess water and put in a large enamel or stainless steel pot; no extra water is required. Place over high heat, cover, and cook until just tender, stirring once or twice. Drain, squeeze dry in a tea towel then chop coarsely.

**4** Heat 4 tablespoons olive oil and gently sauté sultanas and pine nuts until nuts are golden and the sultanas swollen. Add garlic, toss through, then add spinach. Cook, stirring, for 20 to 30 seconds. Season to taste with salt and pepper. Remove from heat, allow to cool 5 minutes then lightly toss through ricotta. The appearance is better if the ricotta remains in clumps throughout the spinach.

**5** Spoon filling onto pizza base, keeping within the rim. Sprinkle fontina over surface and drizzle on a tablespoon of olive oil. Transfer to oven and bake until dough is golden and cheeses bubbling, 20 to 25 minutes.

**MAKES ONE 28 CM (11 IN) PIZZA**

# SCALLOP, ZUCCHINI (COURGETTE) AND BASIL PIZZA

**250 g (8 oz) fresh scallops**

**125 ml (4 fl oz) milk**

**olive oil**

**300 g (10 oz) small zucchini (courgette)**

**salt**

**½ x recipe Cornmeal Dough as for Green Asparagus and Parmesan Pizzette, (see recipe page 30)**

**30 g (1 oz) butter**

**250 g (8 oz) grated mozzarella cheese**

**freshly ground black pepper**

**2 tablespoons grated parmesan cheese mixed with 1 teaspoon finely grated lemon rind**

**1 tablespoon shredded fresh basil leaves**

**1** Cut scallops in half if large, then place in a small bowl to soak with milk and 1 tablespoon olive oil.

**2** Thinly slice zucchini (courgette), place in a colander and sprinkle with salt. Set aside to drain for 15 minutes then shake dry.

**3** Preheat oven to 220°C (425°F) and brush a pizza tray with oil.

**4** Roll and shape dough on a floured surface into a 30 cm (12 in) circle with a raised rim. Transfer to prepared tray, brush surface with olive oil and set aside.

**5** Melt butter in a pan and gently sauté zucchini (courgette) slices until crisply tender. Remove from pan with a slotted spoon and drain on absorbent paper. Drain scallops, add to pan and sauté 3 to 4 minutes. Drain on absorbent paper.

**6** Scatter mozzarella on base, followed by zucchini (courgette) and scallops. Red capsicum (pepper) can also be added (see cover). Season to taste with black pepper and drizzle on 1 to 2 teaspoons of olive oil. Sprinkle parmesan/rind mix and basil over surface.

**7** Transfer to oven and bake until dough is golden, 15 to 18 minutes.

**MAKES ONE 30 CM (12 IN) PIZZA**

**≈ PIZZETTE WITH GOAT'S CHEESE, SUN-DRIED CAPSICUMS (PEPPERS) AND THYME**

*These individual pizzas are very good looking and have a fresh, slightly tangy flavour. The trick to keeping the thyme green and fragrant is to add it for the last 5 minutes of baking only. If sun-dried capsicums (peppers) are unavailable, sun-dried tomatoes marinated in olive oil are almost as good.*

# PIZZETTE WITH GOAT'S CHEESE, SUN-DRIED CAPSICUMS (PEPPERS) AND THYME

**1 x recipe Basic Pizza Dough, (see recipe page 10)**

**olive oil, for brushing**

**600 g (20 oz) fresh tomatoes**

**freshly ground black pepper**

**500 g (16 oz) chevre or other goat's milk cheese**

**30 g (1 oz) drained sun-dried capsicums (peppers) in oil**

**2 tablespoons of marinade oil from sun-dried capsicums mixed with 1 tablespoon extra virgin olive oil**

**24 small sprigs fresh thyme**

**1** Preheat oven to 230°C (450°F) and brush 2 heavy-duty baking trays with oil.

**2** Divide dough into 8 equal pieces and roll or shape each on a floured surface into a 17 cm (6¾ in) circle with a raised rim. Transfer to prepared trays and brush surfaces with olive oil.

**3** Peel and seed tomatoes, then cut flesh into 1 cm (½ in) dice. Season to taste with black pepper.

**4** Crumble cheese or dice into 1 cm (½ in) pieces, depending on texture.

**5** Cut capsicum (pepper) into thin strips of 2 cm (¾ in) length.

**6** Scatter tomatoes and cheese over pizzette bases then arrange capsicum (pepper) strips in a pattern on top. Drizzle marinade/olive oil over surfaces.

**7** Transfer to oven and bake for 10 minutes. Remove and quickly decorate each pizzette with 3 thyme sprigs then return to the oven for a further 5 minutes, or until dough is golden. Serve at once.

**MAKES EIGHT 17 CM (6¾ IN) PIZZETTE**

*Pizzette with Goat's Cheese, Sun-dried Capsicums (Peppers) and Thyme; Scallop, Zucchini (Courgette) and Basil Pizza*

*Pizza Siciliana; Pizza with Prawns (Shrimps), Garlic and Feta*

# PIZZA WITH PRAWNS (SHRIMPS), GARLIC AND FETA

*For this pizza the ingredients are laid down in the opposite order than the usual. This gives a succulent base and is an interesting alternative to melting cheeses on top.*

**1 x recipe Basic Pizza Dough, (see recipe page 10)**

**olive oil**

**500 g (16 oz) (approximately 2 large) fresh tomatoes, peeled, seeded and diced**

**½ teaspoon salt**

**¼ teaspoon sugar**

**2 to 3 garlic cloves, finely minced**

**40 g (1½ oz) butter**

**2 tablespoons olive oil**

**300 g (10 oz) shelled raw prawns (shrimps), deveined and halved lengthwise**

**4 medium leeks, trimmed and thinly sliced**

**freshly ground black pepper**

**350 g (11½ oz) feta cheese, crumbled or cut into 1 cm (½ in) dice**

**4 teaspoons chopped fresh basil**

**1** Preheat oven to 220°C (425°F) and brush 2 baking trays with oil.

**2** Divide dough in half then roll out and shape on a floured surface into 2 rectangles with a slightly raised rim, 8 mm (⅓ in) thick and approximately 22 cm x 36 cm (8¾ in x 14½ in). Transfer to prepared trays and brush surfaces with oil. Set aside, covered with tea towels, until needed.

**3** Toss tomatoes with salt and sugar and place in a colander to drain. Just before use, press out excess liquid and stir in garlic.

**4** Melt butter and 2 tablespoons olive oil in a pan and sauté prawns (shrimps) until just turned opaque, 20 to 25 seconds. Remove with a slotted spoon then drain on absorbent paper. Add leeks to pan and gently sauté until soft. Season to taste with pepper.

**5** Distribute feta over pizza bases. Top with a layer of leeks, then tomatoes. Transfer to oven and bake until dough begins to colour, about 15 minutes.

**6** Arrange prawns on top, drizzle a little olive oil over these and continue baking until dough is golden, a further 3 to 4 minutes. Sprinkle basil over the top and serve at once, cut into squares.

**MAKES 2 RECTANGLES APPROXIMATELY 22 CM X 36 CM (8¾ IN X 14½ IN)**

# PIZZA SICILIANA

**1 x recipe Yeastless Pizza Dough, (see recipe page 11)**

**olive oil, for brushing**

**800 g (26 oz) fresh tomatoes, peeled, seeded and diced**

**1 teaspoon salt**

**½ teaspoon sugar**

**1 garlic clove, finely minced**

**freshly ground black pepper**

**2 tablespoons olive oil**

**250 g (8 oz) provolone cheese, thinly sliced**

**300 g (10 oz) fresh anchovies, cleaned and gutted with heads and bones removed, rubbed with salt**

**olive oil**

**1 teaspoon dried oregano**

**1** Preheat oven to 220°C (425°F) and brush a large pizza tray with oil.

**2** Roll out and shape dough on a floured surface to a large circle 8 mm (⅓ in) thick with a slightly raised rim. Transfer to prepared tray, brush surface with oil and set aside.

**3** Place tomatoes in a colander and force out excess liquid. Transfer to a bowl and add salt, sugar, garlic and season to taste with black pepper. Stir in 2 tablespoons olive oil.

**4** Spread half tomatoes over pizza base then arrange provolone slices on top. Transfer to oven and bake until dough just begins to brown and cheese has melted, about 15 minutes.

**5** Top with remaining tomatoes then arrange anchovies in a spoke-like pattern over this. Drizzle olive oil sparingly over anchovies and sprinkle oregano on top. Bake a further 10 minutes, or until anchovies are cooked and dough is golden.

**MAKES 1 PIZZA OF APPROXIMATELY 38 CM (15 IN) DIAMETER**

**≈ PIZZA SICILIANA**

*In Sicily the pizza is called sfinciuni, a word said to be of Arabic derivation. One train of thought is that the pizza was introduced to Italy by the Arabs in Sicily and it has remained pretty much unchanged on the island. Certainly it takes a more simple form than those from mainland Italy and it is very similar to hearthbreads found in regions of North Africa. Topped with anchovies, tomatoes and cheese it resembles the type of flat open pie found all over the Mediterranean, from Malta and Sardinia to Mallorca.*

**≈ Balearic Pizza**
*Coca de Baleares or Coca de Trampo is a simple, cheeseless pizza found throughout the Balearic Islands to which Mallorca and Ibiza belong. The pizzas are shaped into large rectangles, topped with a good combination of vegetables ('trampo' in Mallorcan) and cut into squares, much the same way as pizza is served in Rome.*

**≈ Pissaladiere**
*From Provence in France, pissaladiere is a close relative to the pizza. It is named from pissala, a puree of salted baby anchovies, but the catching of these in the Mediterranean is now supposed to be outlawed. Anchovy fillets preserved in salt make a good substitute, but first soak them in milk for 15 minutes or so to get rid of excess salt.*

# BALEARIC PIZZA

**1 x recipe Basic Pizza Dough, (see recipe page 10)**

**olive oil for brushing + 3 tablespoons olive oil**

**2 large onions, sliced into rings**

**3 to 4 garlic cloves, minced**

**2 medium red capsicums (peppers), thinly sliced**

**2 x 440 g (14 oz) tins peeled tomatoes, seeds and juice squeezed out and chopped**

**salt and freshly ground black pepper**

**750 g (24 oz) cooked, well drained and chopped spinach**

**2 teaspoons pine nuts**

**24 Niçoise or Ligurean or other small black olives, seeded**

**extra 2 tablespoons olive oil**

**1** Preheat oven to 180°C (350°F) and brush 2 large baking trays with oil.

**2** Divide dough in half. Roll out and shape each on a floured surface to a rectangle of approximately 22 cm x 40 cm (8¾ in x 16 in) with a slightly raised rim. Transfer to prepared trays and brush surfaces with oil.

**3** Heat oil in a large frying pan and gently sauté onion for 10 minutes. Add garlic and red capsicum (pepper), sauté a further 2 to 3 minutes then stir in tomatoes. Season to taste with salt and pepper and cook, stirring from time to time, until sauce loses excess liquid. Remove from heat and stir in spinach. Taste for salt and pepper, adding more if necessary.

**4** Spread mixture over bases evenly, scatter on pine nuts and arrange olives on top. Drizzle extra olive oil over surfaces.

**5** Bake until dough is golden, about 25 minutes. May be served hot or cold, cut into pieces.

**Makes 2 x rectangular pizzas of approximately 22 cm x 40 cm (8¾ in x 16 in)**

# PISSALADIERE

**½ recipe Yeastless Pizza Dough, (see recipe page 11)**

**olive oil, for brushing**

**50 g (2 oz) drained anchovy fillets**

**3 tablespoons milk**

**3 tablespoons olive oil**

**20 g (½ oz) butter**

**600 g (20 oz) onions, thinly sliced**

**salt and freshly ground black pepper**

**50 g (2 oz) stoned black olives, cut in half**

**1** On a floured surface, roll out and shape dough to a circle of 26 cm (10½ in) diameter with a slightly raised rim. Transfer to a pizza or baking tray which has been brushed with oil. Brush dough with oil, cover, and rest 30 minutes.

**2** Preheat oven to 200°C (400°F).

**3** Put anchovies and milk in a small bowl and set aside to soak for 15 minutes. Drain, then slice in half lengthwise.

**4** Heat oil and butter in a heavy-based frying pan. Add onions and gently fry until soft and golden; 12 to 15 minutes. Do not allow to brown. Season to taste with salt and pepper. Spread over dough base, keeping rim free. With the anchovies make a criss-cross pattern over the surface. Place an olive half inside each of the squares created. Transfer to oven and bake 15 minutes, then reduce temperature to 180°C (350°F). Continue baking until golden, about 15 minutes more. May be served warm or at room temperature.

**Makes 1 x 26 cm (10½ in) tart**

*Pissaladiere; Balearic Pizza*

*Deep-dish Seafood Pizza; Armenian Pizza*

# ARMENIAN PIZZA

*Armenian pizzas or lahmajoons are distinguished by their unique combination of flavours. They are usually spicy and invariably contain minced beef or lamb.*

**1 x recipe Yeastless Pizza Dough, (see recipe page 11)**

**1 medium onion, finely chopped**

**1 tablespoon salt**

**1 tablespoon toasted pine nuts**

**450 g (14½ oz) lean minced beef**

**½ teaspoon ground allspice**

**1 teaspoon ground cumin**

**¼ teaspoon cayenne pepper**

**3 tablespoons finely chopped parsley**

**salt and freshly ground black pepper**

**tomato juice, about 4 tablespoons**

**1** Preheat oven to 220°C (425°F) and brush 2 baking trays with oil.

**2** Divide dough in half. By pressing the centre of each flat then working out towards the edges, shape by hand into an oval approximately 18 cm (7 in) wide and 34 cm (13½ in) long. Form a slight rim around the edges. Transfer to baking trays and prick over surfaces with a fork, then cover with tea towels and set aside.

**3** Put onion in a small bowl and toss with salt. Set aside for 15 minutes.

**4** Put pine nuts, beef, allspice, cumin, cayenne and parsley in a large bowl and mix well. Salt and pepper to taste. Squeeze liquid from onions then add them to the bowl. Add tomato juice, one tablespoon at a time, until mixture is just united but not sticky.

**5** Divide mixture in two and spread over bases with the back of a fork. Position in oven one above the other and bake until dough is cooked and pale golden, 12 to 15 minutes. If your oven heats unevenly, bake one tray at a time. Serve at once.

**MAKES 2 X OVAL PIZZAS APPROXIMATELY 18 CM X 34 CM (7 IN X 13½ IN)**

# DEEP-DISH SEAFOOD PIZZA

**1 x recipe Cornmeal Pizza Dough as for Green Asparagus and Parmesan Pizzette, (see recipe page 30)**

**olive oil, for brushing**

**6 thick slices fresh white bread, crusts removed**

**100 ml (3½ fl oz) milk**

**3 tablespoons olive oil**

**20 g (½ oz) butter**

**1 small onion, finely chopped**

**3 tablespoons finely chopped fennel bulb**

**2 garlic cloves, minced**

**250 g (8 oz) peeled uncooked prawns (shrimps)**

**250 g (8 oz) raw scallops, rinsed and trimmed**

**3 tablespoons white wine**

**salt and freshly ground black pepper**

**150 g (5 oz) cooked crab or lobster meat**

**3 to 4 tablespoons chopped parsley**

**3 eggs, lightly beaten**

**1** Preheat oven to 240°C (465°F) and grease two 22 cm (8¾ in) pie tins which have 4 cm to 5 cm (1½ in to 2 in) rims.

**2** Divide dough in half, then, on a floured surface roll out each to a circle of 30 cm (12 in). Rest for 10 minutes, then use to line prepared tins. Level off upper edges and crimp these with the fingers. Prick all over the bases with a fork. Transfer to oven and bake for 5 minutes. Brush the entire inside crust with olive oil and set aside.

**3** In the meantime, place bread in a shallow bowl and cover with milk.

**4** Heat oil and butter in a frying pan and gently sauté onion, fennel and garlic for 6 to 8 minutes. Add prawns (shrimps) and scallops and sauté until just opaque, 1 to 2 minutes. Increase temperature, add wine and wait until it has evaporated before removing pan from heat. Season generously with salt and pepper and toss through crab meat and parsley. Add soaked bread and eggs and stir well so that bread disintegrates. Pour into crusts and transfer to oven, one per oven shelf. After 5 minutes, swap tins around, then after another 5 minutes, reduce temperature to 200°C (400°F). Bake until crust is golden and filling set, a further 20 to 25 minutes.

**MAKES TWO 22 CM (8¾ IN) PIZZAS**

**SERVES 4 AS A MAIN MEAL, 8 AS A SNACK**

**≈ DEEP-DISH SEAFOOD PIZZA**

*The United States of America was possibly the first country outside Italy to have the pizzeria, and indeed had it years before it appeared in the north of Italy. Early migrants from Naples to America established the pizza in their communities and in 1905 the first pizzeria was opened in New York. This deep-dish style was first introduced by the Pizzeria Uno of Chicago in 1941 and has become increasingly popular throughout the country. Special wide pans with 4 cm to 5 cm (1½ to 2 in) rims are available but a shallow-rimmed cake or pie tin will do the trick.*

**≈ Pizza Rustica**

*Pizza rustica is not a classic round, flat pizza, but something much truer to its name, literally farmhouse pie. It has been around Italian country kitchens for hundreds of years and was made with eggs and bits and pieces of other tasty produce.*

# PIZZA RUSTICA

**½ x recipe Yeastless Pizza Dough, (see recipe page 11)**

**4 tablespoons breadcrumbs**

**100 g (3½ oz) lean ham or prosciutto**

**2 eggs**

**150 ml (5 fl oz) cream**

**1 tablespoon grated parmesan cheese**

**pinch nutmeg**

**1 large tomato, skinned and seeded, cut into small pieces**

**80 g (2½ oz) mozzarella cheese, diced**

**2 tablespoons finely chopped parsley**

**2 teaspoons finely chopped fresh oregano, or ½ teaspoon dried**

**freshly ground black pepper**

**50 g (2 oz) shredded emmenthal or fontina cheese**

**1** Preheat oven to 190°C (375°F) and grease a shallow rectangular pie dish approximately 18 cm x 28 cm (7 in x 11 in).

**2** Roll out dough on a floured surface to a rectangle approximately 22 cm x 32 cm (8¾ in x 12¾ in). Rest for 10 minutes, then use to line prepared dish. Neaten edges and prick base with a fork. Sprinkle on breadcrumbs, then layer ham over the top.

**3** In a bowl beat eggs, cream, parmesan and nutmeg. Stir in tomato, mozzarella, parsley and oregano, and season with pepper. Pour over ham in pie dish then sprinkle emmenthal over the top. Transfer to oven and bake until filling is set and dough golden, about 35 minutes. Serve warm.

**Serves 4 as a light meal**

# SPINACH AND SAUSAGE PIZZA

**1 x recipe Yeastless Wholemeal Dough, (see recipe page 11)**

**olive oil for brushing**

**1 tablespoon oil**

**½ small onion, finely chopped**

**400 g (13 oz) raw coarse Italian sausages**

**20 g (½ oz) butter**

**400 g (13 oz) button mushrooms, sliced**

**150 g (5 oz) cooked spinach, chopped and squeezed dry**

**1 teaspoon lemon juice**

**pinch nutmeg**

**salt and freshly ground black pepper**

**200 g (6½ oz) shredded gouda or cheddar cheese**

**2 medium tomatoes, sliced**

**1** Preheat oven to 220°C (425°F) and brush a large pizza or baking tray with oil.

**2** Roll out or shape dough on a floured surface to a 38 cm (15 in) circle with a slightly raised rim. Transfer to prepared tray, brush with olive oil and set aside.

**3** Heat oil in a frying pan and add onion. Remove casings from sausages and crumble filling into pan. Sauté gently for 8 to 10 minutes. Add butter and mushrooms and continue cooking until mushrooms are tender but crisp, stirring often. Remove from heat and stir in spinach, lemon juice, nutmeg, and salt and pepper to taste.

**4** Spread filling over base and sprinkle on two thirds of the cheese. Transfer to oven and bake for 15 minutes. Arrange tomato slices over surface, sprinkle on remaining cheese and return to the oven for another 5 to 10 minutes, or until crust is golden. Cool for 5 minutes before serving.

**Makes one 38 cm (15 in) pizza**

*Spinach and Sausage Pizza; Pizza Rustica*

# THICK PIZZA WITH SUN-DRIED TOMATO PASTE, ARTICHOKES AND PARMESAN

**1 x recipe Basic Pizza Dough, (see recipe page 10)**

**4 to 5 tablespoons sun-dried tomato paste (see Glossary page 95)**

**80 g (2½ oz) grated mozzarella cheese**

**800 g (26 oz) drained tinned artichoke hearts**

**freshly ground black pepper**

**60 g (2 oz) grated good quality parmesan cheese**

**olive oil**

**1** Preheat oven to 250°C (475°F) and brush a pizza or baking tray with oil.

**2** Roll out dough on a floured surface to a circle approximately 25 cm (10 in) across. Stretch with the hands to a diameter of 34 cm to 36 cm (13½ in x 14½ in), forming a slightly raised rim. Transfer to prepared tray.

**3** Spread tomato paste over surface inside the rim, then scatter on mozzarella.

**4** Slice each artichoke heart into four along its length. Arrange slices in an overlapping pattern over mozzarella and season to taste with black pepper. Sprinkle parmesan over the pizza.

**5** Lightly brush outer rim with olive oil, then drizzle 2 to 3 tablespoons over the entire surface.

**6** Transfer to the oven and bake until dough is golden, 20 to 25 minutes.

**MAKES ONE 34 CM (13½ IN) PIZZA**

**≈ GREEN ASPARAGUS AND PARMESAN PIZZETTE WITH CORNMEAL DOUGH**

*Asparagus and parmesan cheese are one of those combinations which must have been made in heaven. The taste is hard to beat and whatever the presentation, the dish is always elegant.*
*In this recipe these two ingredients are further complemented by using a cornmeal dough, but this is not essential.*

# GREEN ASPARAGUS AND PARMESAN PIZZETTE WITH CORNMEAL DOUGH

**CORNMEAL DOUGH**

**3 teaspoons caster sugar**

**85 ml (3 fl oz) warm water (41°C to 42°C/106°F to 108°F comfortable to the fingers)**

**oil, for brushing**

**1 sachet (7 g/¼ oz) active dry yeast**

**250 g (8 oz) plain (baker's/all-purpose) flour**

**215 g (7 oz) fine cornmeal or polenta (instant polenta works well)**

**½ teaspoon salt**

**65 ml (2 fl oz) olive oil**

**170 ml (6 fl oz) warm water, extra, temperature as above**

**TOPPING**

**32 thin fresh asparagus spears**

**olive oil**

**400 g (13 oz) mozzarella cheese, grated**

**250 g (8 oz) parmesan cheese, coarsely grated**

**freshly ground black pepper**

**1** To make Cornmeal Dough, follow instructions for Basic Pizza Dough (see recipe page 10) adding cornmeal to the dry ingredients. After the risen dough has been punched down, divide into 8 equal pieces. Roll out or shape each on a floured surface into a circle 16 cm (6½ in) across with a slightly raised rim. Brush 2 heavy-duty baking trays with oil then position pizzette on them. Brush surfaces with oil.

**2** Preheat oven to 240°C (465°F).

**3** Remove tough ends from asparagus and trim them to no more than 14 cm (5¾ in) long. Keeping 8 whole, cut the remaining spears in half. Place in a shallow bowl and add 4 tablespoons olive oil. Toss by hand to coat well.

**4** Toss the two cheeses together then

istribute over dough bases, leaving the rims lear. Take 1 whole asparagus spear and osition across the centre of pizzette. Then, sing a top on one side of this and a tail on he other, form a cross. Fill in the pattern, ke the spokes of a wheel, with 2 more tops nd tails keeping all the tops on one side. Repeat with remaining pizzette and asparagus. Lightly season with black pepper.

**5** Bake one tray at a time for approximately 12 minutes, or until dough is golden and asparagus crisp but tender.

**MAKES 8 PIZZETTE OF 16 CM (6½ IN) DIAMETER**

*Thick Pizza with Sun-dried Tomato Paste, Artichokes and Parmesan; Green Asparagus and Parmesan Pizzette with Cornmeal Dough*

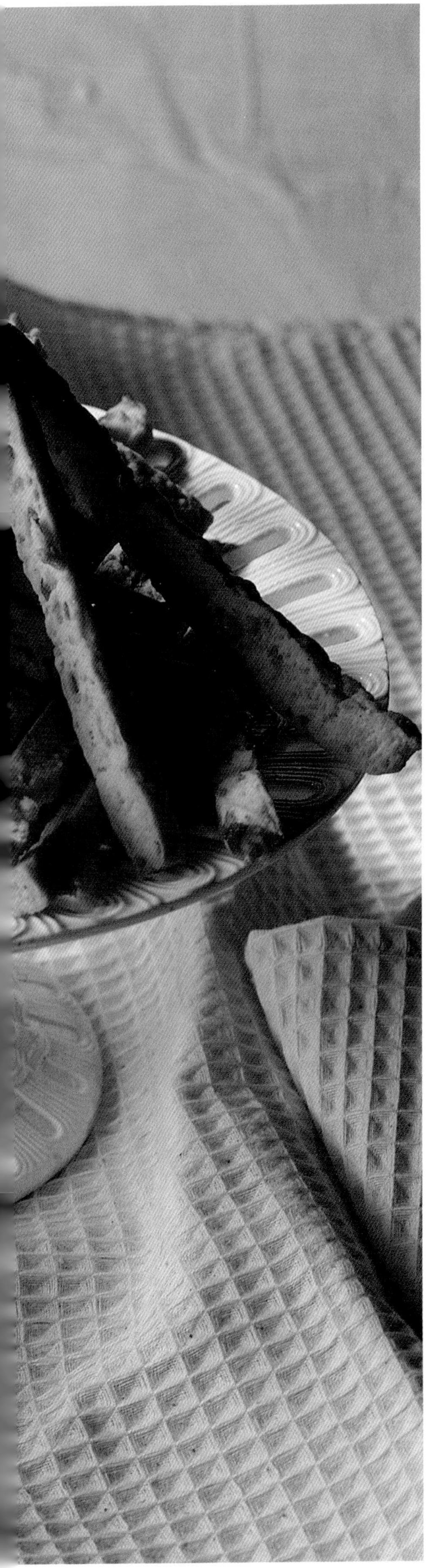

# APPETISERS

It is easy to see how bite-sized breads evolved once you have made a loaf of bread or a pizza and are left with scraps of unused dough. Born out of frugality, these little treats would quickly have become favourites as between meal snacks and their size made them light and easy to transport.

This role is still valid, but now in many countries we are just as likely to make finger food for specific purposes, and they all seem to have something to do with drinking!

*Onion and Black Pepper Grissini (page 34); Mini Panzarotti with Gorgonzola and Walnuts (page 35); Sage and Cream Cheese Bread Sticks (page 34)*

**≈ Sage and Cream Cheese Bread Sticks**

*These crispy sticks are not only ideal to serve with drinks or soup when entertaining at home, but they make a great gift. Any spreadable creamy cheese can be used and a percentage of a soft blue vein cheese gives a particularly good flavour.*

**≈ Onion and Black Pepper Grissini**

*There are many stories as to the origin of the grissini, but a favourite is that a baker in Turin in the 1660s shaped them out of bread dough in response to a request by the local Savoy duke who suffered from indigestion. Grissini made without yeast have the advantage of being very quick to prepare, but their keeping qualities aren't as good. Even stored in an airtight tin they may need to be refreshed in a hot oven before serving.*

# SAGE AND CREAM CHEESE BREAD STICKS

**155 g (5 oz) plain (baker's/all-purpose) flour**

**pinch salt**

**¼ teaspoon paprika**

**60 g (2 oz) butter**

**cold water, to mix**

**60 g (2 oz) soft cream cheese such as bel paese, Mio or Blue Castello**

**1 teaspoon finely chopped fresh sage**

**1** Preheat oven to 200°C (400°F) and grease a baking tray.

**2** This step may be done in a food processor. Put flour, salt and paprika in a bowl and mix well. Rub in butter so that mixture resembles fine breadcrumbs, then add water, a little at a time, to form a stiff dough. Knead lightly. Roll out on a floured surface to a rectangle 5 mm (¼ in) thick. Spread cheese evenly over half the dough and sprinkle sage over this. Fold over the other half to completely cover cheese and sage. Roll out again until 5 mm (¼) thick and the cheese just begins to show through. With a floured knife trim edges, then cut dough into sticks 5 mm (¼ in) wide and as long as you like.

**3** Transfer to prepared tray and bake until lightly browned, about 10 minutes.

**Makes about 50 sticks, depending on length**

# ONION AND BLACK PEPPER GRISSINI

**1 tablespoon olive oil**

**20 g (½ oz) butter**

**1 large onion, finely chopped**

**375 g (12 oz) plain (baker's/all-purpose) flour**

**1 tablespoon baking powder**

**1 teaspoon salt**

**125 g (4 oz) grated parmesan cheese**

**125 g (4 oz) butter, melted and cooled**

**1 large egg**

**125 ml (4 fl oz) warm water**

**1 to 2 teaspoons freshly ground black pepper**

**1** Melt oil and butter in a pan and gently sauté onion. Continue for 12 to 15 minutes until onion is golden, but not brown. Drain on absorbent towelling.

**2** Put flour, baking powder, salt and parmesan in a bowl and mix well. Add butter, egg and water and stir until just combined. This step may be done in a processor up to this point.

**3** Turn dough out onto a floured surface and begin kneading. After 2 minutes begin incorporating black pepper and onion and stop when dough is smooth, 4 to 5 minutes in total. Cover and refrigerate for 30 minutes.

**4** In the meantime preheat oven to 190°C (375°F) and grease then flour a baking tray.

**5** Roll out dough to a rectangle 25 cm x 30 cm (10 in x 12 in) and 8 mm (⅓ in) thick. Using a pastry wheel or a long knife cut rectangle in half along its length, then into strips 8 mm (⅓ in) wide (this will make them 15 cm (6 in) long; however the length can be anything from little shorties to 25 cm (10 in), whatever you prefer). Arrange untouching on prepared tray and bake until golden, 12 to 15 minutes.

**Makes about 50 of 15 cm (6 in) length**

# MINI PANZAROTTI WITH GORGONZOLA AND WALNUTS

**Dough**

**250 g (8 oz) plain (baker's/all-purpose) flour**

**½ teaspoon baking powder**

**1 teaspoon caster sugar**

**½ teaspoon salt**

**1 egg**

**80 ml (2½ fl oz) olive oil**

**1 tablespoon walnut oil (if unavailable, use olive oil)**

**50 ml (2 fl oz) dry white wine**

**Filling**

**450 g (14½ oz) gorgonzola cheese or other creamy blue vein cheese**

**30 g (1 oz) walnuts, roasted then chopped**

**1 egg beaten with 1 tablespoon water, for glazing**

**1 To Prepare Dough:** Put flour, baking powder, sugar and salt in a bowl and mix well. Mix in egg, oils and wine until the dough begins to clump. This may be done in a food processor. Turn out onto a floured surface and complete mixing dough by hand, then knead until smooth and elastic, 3 to 4 minutes. Cover and rest at room temperature for 30 minutes.

**2** Preheat oven to 220°C (425°F) and grease a baking tray.

**3 To Prepare Filling:** Combine gorgonzola and walnuts.

**4** Divide dough in half and roll out each piece to a thickness of 2 mm (⅛ in). Using a cookie cutter cut out 30 circles of 6 cm (2½ in) diameter. The dough scraps can be re-rolled once. Working a few at a time, brush around the rims of dough with beaten egg. Take a scant teaspoon of filling and place in the centre of each circle. Fold dough over to encase filling and press edges together well to seal. Trim edges with a pastry cutter then set aside while finishing off the batch.

**5** Space panzarotti on prepared tray, brush tops with beaten egg and transfer to oven. Bake until golden, approximately 15 minutes.

**Makes approximately 30 mini panzarotti**

# ANCHOVY AND TOMATO PINWHEELS

**180 g (6 oz) leftover bread dough, any kind, or see Pizza Dough base recipes (pages 10, 11)**

**150 g (5 oz) fine textured sausages (pork is good)**

**50 g (2 oz) anchovies, drained and finely chopped**

**1 tablespoon finely chopped parsley**

**1 teaspoon tomato paste**

**1** Roll out dough on a floured surface to a rectangle approximately 24 cm x 32 cm (9½ in x 12¾ in) with a thickness of 3 mm (⅛ in). (Set aside to rest for 10 minutes if using scraps of recently rolled dough.)

**2** To make the filling, squeeze the sausage mince out of skins into a bowl and add anchovies, parsley and tomato paste; mix well.

Spread evenly over dough leaving a 1 cm (½ in) border on one of the long sides uncovered. Brush this edge with water. Starting from the opposite long side, roll dough up jelly roll fashion. Press edge onto the roll to seal. Refrigerate for at least 60 minutes.

**3** Preheat oven to 220°C (425°F) and brush a heavy-duty baking tray with oil.

**4** With a floured knife cut the roll into ½ cm (¼ in) slices. Position these, with space between each one, on prepared tray. Bake until golden, about 15 minutes. Can be served straight from the oven or cold. They will keep for 2 to 3 days if made with a yeast dough; otherwise 24 hours.

**Makes approximately 60 pinwheels**

**≈ Mini Panzarotti with Gorgonzola and Walnuts**

*These little stuffed turnovers can be made with just about any left-over bread dough. They may be made up then frozen, unbaked, or they can be prepared and kept chilled for 24 hours before baking.*

**≈ Anchovy and Tomato Pinwheels**

*Designed to use up left-over dough, pinwheels are fun to make and look great when put out to nibble on with drinks. If a mild anchovy flavour is preferred, the anchovy fillets can be soaked in milk for 15 to 20 minutes before use.*

# CORNBREAD BISCUITS FOR CHEESE

**600 g (20 oz) fine cornmeal (polenta)**

**1 teaspoon salt**

**45 g (1½ oz) pistachio kernels, coarsely chopped**

**150 g (5 oz) butter, melted and cooled**

**1 tablespoon hazelnut or walnut oil**

**3 eggs, lightly beaten**

**375 ml (12 fl oz) milk**

**1** Preheat oven to 180°C (350°F) and grease a 20 cm x 28 cm (8 in x 11 in) baking dish.

**2** Put cornmeal, salt and nuts into a bowl and mix well. Add butter, oil, eggs and just enough milk to make a dough thin enough to be beaten. Beat for 10 minutes. Add remaining milk and beat for another 5 minutes.

**3** Transfer to prepared dish, level surface with the back of a wet spoon and bake until beginning to brown, approximately 20 minutes.

**4** In the meantime, grease a baking tray. Remove bread from oven and cut into small square or diamond shapes about 4 cm x 4 cm (1½ in x 1½ in). Position on baking tray and return to oven until crusty and golden, another 12 to 15 minutes.

**MAKES APPROXIMATELY 35 BISCUITS**

# MOCK TARALLI

**185 g (6 oz) plain (baker's/all-purpose) flour**

**¼ teaspoon baking powder**

**¼ teaspoon salt**

**½ tablespoon sugar**

**1 tablespoon fennel seeds**

**1 egg, lightly beaten**

**75 ml (2½ fl oz) olive oil**

**40 ml (1½ fl oz) dry white wine**

**1 egg beaten with 1 tablespoon water, to glaze**

**1 to 2 tablespoons coarse sea salt**

**1** Put flour, baking powder, salt, sugar and fennel seeds in a bowl and mix well. Add egg, oil and wine and stir with a wooden spoon until mixture starts to clump. Turn out onto a floured surface and finish mixing by hand. Knead for 2 or 3 minutes until smooth and elastic. Rest, uncovered for 10 minutes.

**2** Divide dough in half and roll out each to a rectangle of 16 cm x 32 cm (6½ in x 12¾ in). With a sharp knife cut along each sheet at 1 cm (½ in) intervals, giving thirty two 1 cm (½ in) wide lengths from each piece of dough. Working one at a time, lightly roll strips on the floured surface to form a rounded rope, but try to keep the same length. Twist ends around to meet each other and press together, forming a shape. As each one is finished, position on a lightly oiled baking tray. Cover with a tea towel and rest for 15 minutes.

**3** In the meantime, preheat oven to 200°C (400°F).

**4** Brush taralli with egg/water mix and sprinkle with coarse salt. Bake until golden and crisp, about 12 minutes.

**MAKES 64**

**≈ CORNBREAD BISCUITS FOR CHEESE**

*These 'biscuits' are made from cornbread which is partially baked before being cut into bite-sized pieces and finished off in the oven. They are traditionally served warm with soft or fresh cheeses, but they make a good base for cocktail food when sliced in half and toasted. They may also be flavoured with herbs or other nut varieties.*

**≈ MOCK TARALLI**

*Taralli are small, round, twisted, pretzel-like breads. Traditionally made with yeast and boiled before being baked, we bypass both these time-consuming steps here but still end up with crisp little snacks, just the thing to nibble on with pre-dinner drinks.*

*Cornbread Biscuits for Cheese accompanied here by prosciutto and olives; Mock Taralli*

**≈ MIGAS**

*To say that migas are popular in Spain is an understatement; they are eaten as a snack, as a tapa and served as a crouton with soups. This recipe is perfect as an accompaniment to pre-dinner drinks.*

# BLACK OLIVE AND RED CAPSICUM (PEPPER) DIAMONDS

**500 g (16 oz) plain (baker's/all-purpose) flour**

**2 teaspoons salt**

**1 teaspoon baking powder**

**2 cloves garlic, minced**

**30 g (1 oz) seeded black olives, chopped**

**½ medium red capsicum (pepper), finely chopped**

**100 g (3½ oz) butter, melted**

**500 ml (16 fl oz) milk**

**50 g (2 oz) butter melted, for brushing**

**1** Put flour, salt and baking powder in a bowl and mix well. Add garlic, olives and red capsicum (pepper) and toss to distribute evenly. Pour in butter and milk and stir to form a loose dough. Finish mixing by hand, then knead for 3 to 4 minutes. Place in a plastic bag and chill, at least 30 minutes.

**2** Preheat oven to 200°C (400°F) and brush a 30 cm x 40 cm (12 in x 16 in) baking tray with melted butter.

**3** Roll dough out on a floured surface to a thin sheet the size of the baking tray. Roll dough over rolling pin and transport to tray; position squarely then rest for 10 minutes before proceeding. Trim rough edges and patch any tears. Brush surface with butter. With a pastry wheel, cut dough into strips 2.5 cm to 3 cm (1 in to 1¼ in) wide. Then cut diagonally through these to give diamond-shaped pieces.

**4** Transfer to oven and bake until golden, about 6 minutes. Depending on the oven, it may be necessary to turn the diamonds with an egg slice if they brown more quickly on the underside. Allow to cool before serving.

**MAKES APPROXIMATELY 100 DIAMONDS**

# MIGAS

**1 loaf of country-style white bread, 1 or 2 days old (choose a loaf with a solid texture, not with air pockets)**

**1 to 2 teaspoons salt**

**a little cold water**

**olive oil, for frying**

**2 cloves garlic, minced**

**1 teaspoon cumin seeds**

**180 g (6 oz) garlic salami, cut into 1 cm (½ in) cubes**

**1 tablespoon finely chopped fresh coriander**

**1** Remove crusts from bread and cut it into small cubes about 1 cm (½ in) square. Toss bread in a bowl with salt then sprinkle on a little cold water (just enough to moisten; the bread shouldn't become soggy). Wrap in a tea towel and leave for at least 3 hours.

**2** Put olive oil in a frying pan to a depth of 3 mm (⅛ in) and place over a moderate heat. Add garlic and cumin seeds, fry about 20 seconds then add bread and salami. Fry, stirring, until bread is golden on all sides. Drain on absorbent towels before serving, garnished with coriander.

**SERVES 6 TO 8 AS AN ACCOMPANIMENT TO DRINKS**

# CHICKEN IN A CARRIAGE

**DOUGH**

**250 g (8 oz) plain (baker's/all-purpose) flour**

**½ teaspoon baking powder**

**½ teaspoon salt**

**1 teaspoon caster sugar**

**1 egg**

**80 ml (2½ fl oz) olive oil**

**1 tablespoon walnut or hazelnut oil**

**50 ml (2 fl oz) dry white wine**

**FILLING**

**40 g (1½ oz) butter**

**1 tablespoon olive oil**

**1 medium onion, finely chopped**

**400 g (13 oz) lean chicken meat, diced**

**salt and freshly ground black pepper**

**¼ teaspoon cinnamon**

**½ teaspoon ground cardamom**

**juice of ½ lemon**

**30 g (1 oz) pine nuts, toasted**

**1 egg beaten with 1 tablespoon water, to glaze**

**paprika**

**1 To Prepare Dough:** Put flour, baking powder, salt and sugar in a bowl and mix well. Add egg, olive oil, walnut oil and wine and stir until mixture starts to clump around the spoon. Turn out onto a floured surface and finish mixing by hand, then knead for 3 to 4 minutes until smooth. Rest at room temperature for 30 minutes.

**2** Preheat oven to 220°C (425°F) and grease a baking tray.

**3 To Prepare Filling:** Heat butter and oil in a frying pan. Add onion and gently sauté until soft, about 10 minutes. Add chicken meat, season with salt and pepper and sauté 5 minutes. Add cinnamon, cardamom and lemon juice and continue cooking until chicken is tender, about 10 minutes. The mixture needs to be quite dry so increase heat and reduce quickly if you have excess liquid in the pan. Toss through pine nuts, taste for salt and pepper and cool.

**4** Divide dough in half and roll each out into a rectangle 20 cm x 30 cm (8 in x 12 in). Cut each into six 10 cm (4 in) squares and brush around their edges with egg/water. Place approximately 1 tablespoon filling in the centre of each square. Fold one corner over filling, followed by the opposite corner and then the third and fourth corners to form an envelope shape. Press gently to seal then brush tops with egg/ water. Transfer to prepared tray and bake until golden, 15 to 18 minutes. Cool slightly and sprinkle paprika on top before serving.

**Makes 12 parcels**

# PIZZELLE FRITTE WITH MOZZARELLA AND GREEN OLIVES

**500 g (16 oz) bread dough, any kind, or see Pizza Dough base recipes (pages 10, 11)**

**4 tablespoons green olive pâté, or 18 green olives, seeded and chopped**

**250 g (8 oz) mozzarella cheese, cut into small dice**

**18 small fresh basil leaves**

**freshly ground black pepper**

**1 egg, beaten**

**olive oil, for frying**

**1** Divide dough in half and roll each out on a floured surface to a thickness of 2 mm (⅛ in). Rest 10 minutes, then cut out 18 circles of 8 cm (3 in) diameter.

**2** Spread some olive pâté in the centre of each circle, or distribute chopped olives. Place some mozzarella in the middle and then a basil leaf. Season lightly with black pepper. Brush rims with beaten egg then fold circles over on themselves to form a half moon shape. Press and seal edges well. Chill, uncovered, for 10 minutes.

**3** Put olive oil in a frying pan to a depth of 2 cm (¾ in) and heat. When oil begins to shimmer, toss in a small piece of dough. The oil is ready when the dough sizzles and floats on the surface. Fry pizzelle, a few at a time, until puffed and golden on each side. Remove and drain on absorbent paper before serving hot.

**Makes 18 pizzelle**

**≈ Pizzelle Fritte with Mozzarella and Green Olives**

*Like many small bite-sized breads, pizzelle are an example of a by-product becoming very popular in its own right. Using pieces of leftover dough folded around a tasty morsel (probably leftovers as well) pizzelle are fried and served hot.*

*Pizzelle Fritte with Mozzarella and Green Olive (page 39); Sesame Breads*

# SESAME BREADS

**250 g (8 oz) plain (baker's/all-purpose) flour**
**2 teaspoons baking powder**
**1 teaspoon bicarbonate of soda**
**½ teaspoon salt**
**120 g (4 oz) chilled butter, cut into small pieces**
**2 eggs**
**1 tablespoon honey**
**1 teaspoon sesame oil**
**80 ml (2½ fl oz) buttermilk**
**approximately 4 tablespoons sesame seeds**

**≈ SESAME BREADS**
*These fan-shaped breads can be eaten as a snack, served with soup or used as a biscuit for cheese.*

**1** Preheat oven to 220°C (425°F) and position oven racks to accommodate 2 trays. Grease 2 baking trays with butter or margarine.

**2** Put flour, baking powder, bicarbonate of soda and salt into a bowl and mix well. Rub in butter so that mixture resembles coarse meal. Add eggs, honey, sesame oil and buttermilk and mix with a wooden spoon. Add a little more flour or buttermilk to give a manageable, but slightly sticky dough.

**3** Divide dough in half and shape each into a circle 1 cm (½ in) thick. Sprinkle half the sesame seeds on top then transfer to prepared trays, seed sides down. Sprinkle on remaining seeds and lightly press them in. The surfaces don't have to be even; they should be gently contoured. With a sharp knife dipped in flour, make a spoke-like pattern on the tops, dividing each circle into 8 wedges. Cut through about half way as the breads are to be snapped into sections once baked.

**4** Transfer to oven and bake until golden, 12 to 15 minutes. Cool on wire racks and when ready to serve break into wedges.

**MAKES 16 PIECES**

*Crostini with Cheese, Olive and Tomato Topping (page 42); Crostini with Chicken Liver Topping served with antipasto (page 42)*

**≈ CROSTINI**

*Crostini are small toasts with a topping, served as hors d'oeuvres. They are native to Tuscany and were originally topped with a unique chicken liver mixture, but now there are any number of different toppings to choose from. Here is an original recipe, plus a more modern one.*

# CROSTINI

**1 thin Italian baguette or sfilatino**

**approximately 6 tablespoons extra virgin olive oil**

Leaving the crust on, cut baguette into 40 slices 6 mm to 8 mm (¼ in to ⅓ in) thick. Brush each side lightly with oil, then grill, bake or fry them on a griddle until pale gold. Cool, then spoon on topping just before serving so that the toasts remain crisp.

# CROSTINI WITH CHICKEN LIVER TOPPING

**60 g (2 oz) butter**

**4 tablespoons finely chopped onion**

**1 garlic clove, minced**

**400 g (13 oz) chicken livers, cleaned and trimmed**

**1 bay leaf**

**4 tablespoons Marsala**

**freshly ground black pepper**

**3 anchovy fillets, drained and finely chopped**

**1½ teaspoons tiny capers, optional**

**1 tablespoon finely chopped parsley**

**1** Heat butter in a frying pan and gently sauté onion for 5 minutes. Add garlic, sauté 15 to 20 seconds, then stir in chicken livers. Sauté until livers are browned, about 5 minutes, then add bay leaf, Marsala and black pepper to taste. Increase heat and cook, stirring, until most of the liquid has evaporated.

**2** Remove livers from pan and chop finely. Don't use a processor, as the texture should be coarse, not puréed. Return to pan along with anchovies, capers and parsley and sauté until amalgamated, about 1 minute. Remove bay leaf. Serve warm, spread on crostini.

**ENOUGH FOR APPROXIMATELY 40 SMALL TOASTS OR 8 LARGE ENTREE SIZE TOASTS**

# CHEESE, OLIVE AND TOMATO TOPPING

**400 g (13 oz) provolone or emmenthal cheese, thinly sliced**

**10 large cherry tomatoes, cut into four**

**20 stuffed green olives (can be stuffed with red capsicum (pepper), almond or anchovies), cut in half lengthwise**

**freshly ground black pepper**

**dried oregano or chopped fresh, about 1 tablespoon**

**approximately 2 tablespoons extra virgin olive oil**

**1** Preheat griller to moderately hot.

**2** Cover toasts with a slice of cheese. Place a tomato piece in the middle and an olive half on top of this. Season with black pepper and sprinkle oregano sparingly over the top. Drizzle on a little olive oil, then transfer to baking trays. Position under griller and toast until cheese has melted and is lightly golden. Serve at once.

**MAKES APPROXIMATELY 40 SMALL TOASTS**

# WHOLEMEAL CHEESE AND BEER STICKS

**185 g (6 oz) (baker's/all-purpose) flour**
**230 g (7½ oz) wholemeal flour**
**1 tablespoon baking powder**
**1 teaspoon salt**
**125 g (4 oz) grated pecorino cheese**
**125 ml (4 fl oz) butter, melted and cooled**
**1 egg**
**140 ml (4½ fl oz) beer, not flat**
**extra 30 g (1 oz) grated pecorino cheese**

**1** This step may be done in a processor. Put flours, baking powder, salt and 125 g (4 oz) pecorino in a bowl and mix well. Add butter, egg and beer and stir until a loose dough forms. Turn out onto a floured surface and finish mixing by hand, then knead until smooth. Cover and refrigerate for 30 minutes.
**2** Preheat oven to 190°C (375°F). Grease, then flour 2 baking trays.
**3** Roll dough out to a rectangle approximately 20 cm x 35 cm (8 in x 14 in) and 8 mm (⅓ in) thick. Sprinkle extra pecorino evenly over the surface then lightly press in with another roll of the rolling pin. With a sharp knife or pastry wheel cut dough in half along its length to give 2 pieces of 10 cm (4 in) width. Now cut these into strips 8 mm (⅓ in) wide. Take each strip by its ends and twist it twice before placing on prepared tray. The first few may be warped, but you will quickly develop a nifty technique! Transfer to oven and bake until golden, 12 to 15 minutes. When cool, store in containers.

**MAKES APPROXIMATELY 100 STICKS**

# MITILUGGHIA WITH GARLIC AND WHITE WINE

**125 g (4 oz) plain (baker's/all-purpose) flour**
**pinch salt**
**80 ml (2½ fl oz) warm water**
**2 tablespoons dry white wine**
**1 to 2 cloves garlic, finely chopped**
**olive oil, for frying**

**1** Put flour and salt in a bowl and stir to combine. Add water and wine and work in with a fork until mixture begins to clump. Turn out onto a floured surface and continue mixing by hand. Add more flour or warm water if necessary to give a soft but dry dough. Add garlic and knead until dough is smooth. Divide into 10 equal pieces then roll each out to a thin circle 1 mm (1/16 in) thick. Don't be too worried about shaping the perfect circle! Set aside to rest while oil is heating.
**2** Pour oil into a pan to a depth of 3 cm (1¼ in) and heat. When it begins to shimmer, toss in a small piece of dough. If it bubbles quickly to the top, the oil is hot enough.
**3** Working one at a time, fry until golden. This should take about 10 seconds on the first side and another 5 seconds on the flip side. Drain on paper towels, sprinkle with salt if desired, and serve immediately.

**MAKES 10 MITILUGGHIA**

**≈ MITILUGGHIA WITH GARLIC AND WHITE WINE**

*Mitilugghia are little fried pizzas from Sicily, a legacy of the occupation by Arabs from North Africa. They are nothing more than fried circles of unleavened dough but here they are given a whole new appeal by a subtle flavouring of garlic and wine.*

# ANCHOVY FRIED BUNS

*Just the thing to serve with vegetable soups.*

**60 g (2 oz) anchovy fillets**

**3 tablespoons milk**

**500 g (16 oz) bread dough of choice, but yeasted is best, or see Pizza Dough base recipes (page 10)**

**2 tablespoons chopped parsley**

**oil for deep-frying**

**1** Put anchovies and milk in a small bowl and soak for 20 minutes. Drain and chop coarsely.

**2** On a floured surface flatten dough to a fat circle approximately 15 cm (6 in) across. Spread anchovies over surface and sprinkle on parsley. Fold dough over, press it down firmly, and then repeat folding and pressing 12 times. Rest dough, covered, for 30 minutes.

**3** Roll dough out on the floured surface to a rectangle 1 cm (½ in) thick. Cut into oblong pieces approximately 5 cm x 8 cm (2 in x 3 in).

**4** Heat oil in a deep-fryer to a temperature of 180°C (350°F). If using oil in a saucepan, you will need it at least 4 cm (1½ in) deep. The oil is hot enough when a small piece of dough dances on the surface. Fry buns, 3 to 4 at a time, until golden on both sides. It will only take 3 to 4 minutes. Drain on paper towels and serve at once.

**MAKES APPROXIMATELY 10 BUNS**

# SMOKED SALMON, BRIE AND CAPERS PANZAROTTI

**1 batch Olive Oil and White Wine Dough, (see recipe page 84)**

**125 g (4 oz) dry ricotta cheese**

**200 g (6½ oz) under-ripe brie, rind removed, cut into small dice**

**100 g (3½ oz) smoked salmon, cut into pieces**

**1 teaspoon tiny capers**

**18 small sprigs fresh dill**

**1 egg, lightly beaten**

**1** Preheat oven to 190°C (375°F) and brush a baking tray with oil.

**2** Divide dough in half and roll each out to a thickness of 2 mm (⅛ in). Using an 8 cm (3 in) cookie cutter, cut out 18 circles. The dough scraps can be re-rolled once.

**3** To make the filling, combine ricotta, brie, smoked salmon and capers. Fold in half the egg. To the remaining egg stir in 1 tablespoon milk and set aside for glazing.

**4** Place a teaspoon of filling in the centre of each circle of dough. Brush rims with egg/milk mix then fold one side over the other to encase filling. Press rims together firmly and trim them, then transfer to prepared tray. Brush tops with egg/milk and rest for 15 minutes before baking. Transfer to oven and bake until golden, 12 to 15 minutes. Garnish with dill. May be served hot or at room temperature.

**MAKES 18 PANZAROTTI**

**≈ SMOKED SALMON, BRIE AND CAPERS PANZAROTTI**

*An elegant finger food, these little parcels rely on good quality produce. When heating smoked salmon there is a danger that it will become over salty so choose one with a subtle flavour.*

*nchovy Fried Buns; Smoked Salmon, Brie and apers Panzarotti*

**≈ Spanish French Toast**

*This might sound slightly daffy, but in the northern provinces of Spain torrijas (what we know as French toast) are very popular. This savoury version is eaten hot as an accompaniment to wine. For a less spicy toast, omit paprika and beat eggs with 2 tablespoons green olive pâté.*

# SPANISH FRENCH TOAST

**oil for frying**

**¼ teaspoon paprika**

**250 ml (8 fl oz) milk**

**8 thick slices white bread**

**2 eggs, lightly beaten**

**1** Put oil in a frying pan and heat.

**2** Whisk paprika with milk, then pour into a flat bowl.

**3** Briefly soak bread slices on both sides in the milk. Shake off excess then dip into beaten egg. Shake off excess.

**4** Fry in hot oil, one or two at a time, until golden on both sides. Serve at once, cut into fingers or triangles.

**Enough for 6 to 8 people**

# SEEDED CHEESE FINGERS

**125 g (4 oz) butter at room temperature**

**2 teaspoons hot water**

**185 g (6 oz) plain (baker's/all-purpose) flour**

**60 g (2 oz) shredded mature cheddar or gouda cheese**

**¼ teaspoon curry powder**

**1 egg, beaten with 1 tablespoon milk**

**5 tablespoons sesame seeds**

**5 tablespoons poppy seeds**

**1** Beat butter until pale and thin, gradually incorporating hot water. Add flour and mix to form a smooth dough. Stir in cheese and curry powder. Refrigerate until stiff enough to handle, approximately 60 minutes.

**2** In the meantime, preheat oven to 190°C (375°F) and grease a baking tray.

**3** Break off pieces of dough and roll each into a rope of 1 cm (½ in) diameter. Cut these into 5 cm (2 in) lengths. Brush with egg mixture then roll half the batch in sesame seeds, half in poppy seeds.

**4** Place 2 cm (¾ in) apart on prepared tray and bake until firm and golden, 12 to 15 minutes.

**Makes approximately 40 fingers**

# BACON BARS

**6 rashers bacon**

**250 g (8 oz) plain (baker's/all-purpose) flour**

**1 tablespoon baking powder**

**½ teaspoon salt**

**60 g (2 oz) butter**

**180 ml (6 fl oz) milk**

**1** Preheat oven to 220°C (425°F) and lightly dust a baking tray with flour.

**2** Fry bacon until crisp, remove from pan and drain on paper towels. Cool, then crumble. Reserve 2 tablespoons bacon fat from pan.

**3** In a bowl put flour, baking powder and salt and stir well. Cut in butter until mix resembles coarse breadcrumbs. Add milk and bacon fat and work with a fork until dough just begins to clump. Turn out onto a floured surface, add bacon and knead briefly until uniform in texture. Roll out or pat dough to a rectangle 16 cm x 26 cm (6½ in x 10½ in). Using a floured knife cut into strips every 2 cm (¾ in) along the length. Now cut these in half. Transfer to prepared tray at 2 cm (¾ in) intervals and bake until golden, approximately 10 minutes.

**MAKES 26 BARS**

# BRUSCHETTA

**4 slices country bread (don't remove crusts), about 1 cm (½ in) thick**

**2 garlic cloves, halved and with centre green stem removed**

**salt and freshly ground black pepper**

**approximately 4 tablespoons extra virgin olive oil**

Toast bread on both sides under a grill. While still hot, rub the upper sides well with a garlic half. Sprinkle with salt and pepper, then drizzle over approximately 1 tablespoon olive oil per slice. Serve at once.

**SERVES 4**

**≈ BRUSCHETTA**

*Called bruschetta around Rome, fettunta or fregolotta in Tuscany and soma d'ai in the Piemonte, this classic combination of bread, olive oil and garlic has been enjoyed for hundreds of years. One would be forgiven for thinking that it is unique to Italy, but very similar toasts are eaten in Greece, France and in particular, Spain. Good bruschetta relies on the quality of the olive oil and the amount of garlic used; the former can never be too good while the latter should be restrained.*

# LOAVES AND ROLLS

This chapter contains a great selection of easy breads: some with yeast, most without; some best when served warm, others better after a few hours; some to take on picnics and others to serve at a dinner party; some baked in loaf tins while others are shaped by hand.

For a crustier crust on your loaf, brush the tin with oil instead of greasing with butter or margarine. In those recipes where plain flour and baking powder are used in the proportion of 125 g (4 oz) flour to 1 teaspoon baking powder, self-raising flour may be substituted for plain flour and the baking powder omitted.

*Potato Bread with Bacon and Onion (page 53); Soda Bread with Chives and Fennel (page 53); Tomato and Rosemary Rolls (page 54)*

*Mint and Cheese Picnic Loaf; Rosemary Cornbread*

# MINT AND CHEESE PICNIC LOAF

**6 eggs**

**250 g (8 oz) cheddar cheese, cut into 1 cm (½ in) cubes**

**250 ml (8 fl oz) milk**

**1 tablespoon chopped fresh mint**

**freshly ground black pepper**

**500 g (16 oz) plain (baker's/all-purpose) flour**

**4 teaspoons baking powder**

**1½ teaspoons salt**

**1** Preheat oven to 180°C (350°F) and grease a large deep-sided loaf tin.

**2** Lightly beat eggs in a large bowl. Stir in cheese, then add milk, mint and black pepper to taste. Mix well.

**3** Stir in flour, baking powder and salt and beat until well combined.

**4** Spread mixture in prepared tin, pushing it down firmly with the back of a spoon dipped in cold water. Tap tin hard 3 or 4 times on the bench to settle dough.

**5** Transfer to oven and bake until golden brown and hollow sounding when tapped.

'his should take approximately 40 minutes.
. Allow to cool slightly before turning out nto a wire rack. Serve in thick slices as an ccompaniment to barbecued meats or cold uts.

**Makes 1 loaf approximately 24 cm x 12 cm (9½ in x 5 in), or 2 loaves 8 cm x 18 cm (3 in x 7 in)**

# ROSEMARY CORNBREAD

**150 ml (5 fl oz) milk**

**50 ml (2 fl oz) cold pressed vegetable oil eg corn or Canola**

**2 eggs**

**155 g (5 oz) wholemeal flour**

**130 g (4½ oz) fine cornmeal (polenta)**

**3 teaspoons baking powder**

**pinch salt**

**1 tablespoon chopped fresh rosemary**

**2 to 3 sprigs fresh rosemary**

**1** Preheat oven to 190°C (375°F) and grease a 10 cm x 20 cm (4 in x 8 in) loaf tin.

**2** Combine milk, oil and eggs in a bowl and beat well. Add flour, cornmeal, baking powder, salt and chopped rosemary and mix thoroughly.

**3** Transfer to prepared tin, smooth surface and decorate with rosemary sprigs. Knock tin hard on the bench once or twice to settle dough.

**4** Bake until golden and hollow sounding when tapped, approximately 45 minutes.

**5** Turn out onto a wire rack, cool for 10 to 15 minutes and serve warm or at room temperature, buttered.

**Makes one 10 cm x 20 cm (4 in x 8 in) loaf**

**≈ Rosemary Cornbread**

*This bread is at its best served warm, thinly sliced and buttered. An added bonus is that it makes excellent stuffing for roast meats.*

*Pesto Griddle Cakes*

**≈ Pesto Griddle Cakes**

*Flavoured with pesto, these great little buns are cooked on top of the stove. They can also be done on top of the barbecue or in a kettle type outdoor cooker. The recipe may be made as one large cake to be broken into segments when served.*

# PESTO GRIDDLE CAKES

**250 g (8 oz) plain (baker's/all-purpose) flour**
**½ teaspoon bicarbonate of soda**
**¼ teaspoon salt**
**1 teaspoon sugar**
**125 g (4 oz) butter, cut into pieces**
**1 egg**
**125 ml (4 fl oz) buttermilk or yoghurt**
**2 tablespoons pesto (home-made or ready-made available in supermarkets and delicatessens)**

**1** Put flour, bicarbonate of soda, salt and sugar in a bowl and mix well. Rub in butter so that mixture resembles breadcrumbs. Add egg and buttermilk and stir until mix clumps around the spoon.

**2** Transfer to a floured surface and knead to form a smooth ball. Add pesto, kneading it into dough lightly so that it is swirled through rather than uniformly mixed in. Stop kneading as soon as pesto is absorbed.

**3** Form dough into a ball then roll out to a circle 1 cm (½ in) thick. Cut out rounds with a 5 cm (2 in) cookie cutter or an inverted glass. The trimmings can be rolled out and cut once more before discarding.

**4** In the meantime brush a cast-iron griddle or heavy-duty frying pan with oil and heat over a moderate flame. Cook, a few at a time, until browned, approximately 10 minutes per side. If they cook too fast a hard crust will form and they may burn, so keep checking them. As the cakes are done, transfer to a wire rack to slightly cool before breaking open and buttering.

**Makes 8 to 10 small cakes, or 1 x 20 cm (8 in) cake**

# POTATO BREAD WITH BACON AND ONION

**40 g (1½ oz) butter**

**125 g (4 oz) finely chopped bacon**

**125 g (4 oz) finely chopped onion**

**220 g (7 oz) plain (baker's/all-purpose) flour**

**¼ teaspoon salt**

**2 teaspoons baking powder**

**1 teaspoon sugar**

**½ cup cold mashed potato (approximately 1 large potato)**

**125 ml (4 fl oz) milk**

**2 eggs, beaten**

**1** Preheat oven to 190°C (375°F) and grease an 8 cm x 18 cm (3 in x 7 in) loaf tin.

**2** Melt butter in a frying pan and gently sauté bacon and onion until golden, about 10 minutes. Remove from pan with a slotted spoon and drain on paper towels.

**3** In a bowl combine flour, salt, baking powder and sugar. Add mashed potato, milk and eggs and mix well. Stir through bacon/onion mixture.

**4** Spoon into prepared tin. Pack down well then knock tin against the kitchen bench once or twice to help mixture settle.

**5** Transfer to oven and bake until golden and hollow sounding when tapped, about 45 minutes.

**6** Turn out of tin at once and cool completely before serving.

**MAKES ONE 8 CM X 18 CM (3 IN X 7 IN) LOAF**

# SODA BREAD WITH CHIVES AND FENNEL

**375 g (12 oz) plain (baker's/all-purpose) flour**

**125 g (4 oz) wholemeal flour**

**½ teaspoon bicarbonate of soda**

**½ teaspoon salt**

**1 tablespoon finely chopped chives**

**½ tablespoon fennel seeds**

**300 ml (10 fl oz) buttermilk**

**1** Preheat oven to 200°C (400°F). Brush a 24 cm (9½ in) cast iron pot or Dutch oven with oil and place in the oven to warm for 10 minutes.

**2** Put flours, bicarbonate of soda, salt, chives and fennel seeds in a large bowl and mix well with a wooden spoon. Add three quarters of the buttermilk and work into dry ingredients. Continue to add remaining buttermilk until a soft but kneadable dough forms. Knead with floured hands until smooth, 3 to 4 minutes, then shape into a round loaf.

**3** Transfer to heated pot, flatten slightly then cut a cross in the surface centre with a sharp floured knife. Cover pot with its lid or aluminium foil, transfer to oven and bake for 30 minutes. Remove lid and continue baking until bread is golden and hollow sounding when tapped, a further 10 minutes or so.

**4** Remove with a tea towel and cool on a wire rack for 1 hour before slicing or breaking.

**MAKES 1 LOAF OF UP TO 24 CM (9½ IN) DIAMETER**

**≈ POTATO BREAD WITH BACON AND ONION**

*Potato breads are a great way of using leftover mashed potatoes, and you can often flavour them with other bits and pieces left uneaten after a meal, such as salami or ham. They have a moist texture and the flavour gets better if the loaf is left to sit for a few hours after baking.*

**≈ SODA BREAD WITH CHIVES AND FENNEL**

*Soda bread gets its unique flavour from the interaction of two of the ingredients, bicarbonate of soda and soured milk. Bicarbonate of soda is a good leavening agent but being alkaline, it has an unpleasant soapy taste. To counter this an acid is needed and sour milk, cultured buttermilk or yoghurt fills this role. Buttermilk is particularly good to use, not only for its inherent flavour but also for its consistency which gives a well-textured bread.*

**≈ Tomato and Rosemary Rolls**

*The end result here really justifies the extra effort required with using yeast. The yeasty flavour complements that of tomatoes and garlic, and the extra shelf life made possible by using yeast develops the flavour even more.*

# TOMATO AND ROSEMARY ROLLS

**1 teaspoon sugar**

**3 tablespoons warm water, comfortable to the fingers (41°C to 42°C/106°F to 108°F)**

**1 sachet (7 g/¼ oz) active dry yeast**

**470 g (15 oz) plain (baker's/all-purpose) flour**

**2 teaspoons salt**

**60 ml (2 fl oz) olive oil**

**250 ml (8 fl oz) warm water (comfortable to the fingers)**

**3 to 4 garlic cloves, finely chopped**

**1½ tablespoons tomato paste mixed with 1 teaspoon warm water**

**1 teaspoon chopped fresh rosemary leaves**

**1 tablespoon whole fresh rosemary leaves**

**1** Mix sugar and 3 tablespoons water in a small bowl. Stir in yeast and set aside until foaming; 6 to 8 minutes.

**2** Put flour and salt in a large bowl, stir to blend then add olive oil, 250 ml (8 fl oz) water and the yeast mixture. Stir until mix clumps around the spoon, then transfer to a floured surface.

**3** Knead until a finger imprint springs back out; 8 to 10 minutes.

**4** Place dough in an oiled bowl, roll it around several times to coat the surface then cover tightly with plastic wrap or a plastic bag. Rest in a protected spot until doubled in volume; about 1 hour.

**5** Punch the dough several times to cause it to collapse, then knead in garlic, tomato paste and chopped rosemary leaves. Divide into 12 equal pieces, shape each into a ball and position in a ring, just touching, on an oiled baking tray. Slide into a large plastic bag and set aside to rise again. They are sufficiently risen when a finger imprint remains and doesn't spring back out, about 45 minutes.

**6** In the meantime, preheat oven to 200°C (400°F).

**7** Sprinkle whole rosemary leaves over rolls, gently pressing them in while at the same time flattening the dough slightly. Transfer to oven and bake until golden and hollow sounding when tapped, about 20 minutes. Cool on wire rack before breaking.

**Makes 12 rolls**

# FIG AND PECAN LOAF

**125 g (4 oz) wholemeal flour**

**125 g (4 oz) plain (baker's/all-purpose) flour**

**2 teaspoons baking powder**

**½ teaspoon cinnamon**

**¼ teaspoon cloves**

**1 tablespoon brown sugar**

**60 g (2 oz) butter or margarine**

**60 g (2 oz) pecan halves**

**125 g (4 oz) dried figs, finely chopped**

**60 ml (2 fl oz) beer**

**60 ml (2 fl oz) milk**

**1 egg**

**1** Preheat oven to 190°C (375°F) and grease a 10 cm x 22 cm (4 in x 8¾ in) loaf tin.

**2** Put flours, baking powder, cinnamon, cloves and sugar into a large bowl and mix well. Rub in butter until mixture resembles breadcrumbs. Add pecans and figs; mix well. Add beer, milk and egg and mix to form a soft dough. Turn out onto a floured surface and knead until smooth.

**3** Transfer to prepared tin then flatten and smooth surface with a wet spoon. Place in oven and bake for 10 minutes. Reduce heat to 180°C (350°F) and bake until golden and hollow sounding when tapped, about 30 minutes more. Serve buttered, or with cheese.

**Makes one 10 cm x 22 cm (4 in x 8¾ in) loaf**

*Fig and Pecan Loaf served with che*

**≈ Mini Cheese and Salami Loaves**

*If small loaf tins are unavailable, 4 loaves can still be baked in one large 12 cm x 23 cm (5 in x 9 in) tin. Cut 4 cardboard dividers 12 cm (5 in) long and as tall as the tin, cover them with aluminium foil and use to separate the 4 rolls of dough positioned alongside each other in the tin. It doesn't matter if parts of the dough are touching and bake together; just break the loaves apart like bread rolls once they have cooled.*

# MINI CHEESE AND SALAMI LOAVES

**155 g (5 oz) wholemeal flour**

**250 g (8 oz) plain (baker's/all-purpose) flour**

**3 teaspoons baking powder**

**1 teaspoon salt**

**2 teaspoons dry mustard**

**90 g (3 oz) butter or margarine**

**2 tablespoons good quality grated parmesan cheese**

**90 g (3 oz) finely chopped salami, rind cut off first**

**1 egg, beaten**

**285 ml (9½ fl oz) milk**

**1 tablespoon sesame seeds**

**4 tablespoons grated cheddar cheese**

**1** Preheat oven to 190°C (375°F) and grease 4 mini loaf tins 6 cm x 12 cm (2½ in x 5 in).

**2** Put flours, baking powder, salt and mustard into a bowl and mix well. Rub in butter until mixture resembles fine breadcrumbs. Add parmesan cheese and salami, mix well. Add egg and milk and mix until dough begins to clump around spoon.

**3** Turn out onto floured surface and knead until a smooth dough forms. Divide into 4 equal parts then shape each into a roll the approximate size of the tins. Transfer to tins. Sprinkle sesame seeds and cheddar over the tops then press dough down to mould snugly to the tin shape.

**4** Bake for 10 minutes then reduce temperature to 180°C (350°F). Bake for a further 20 minutes, or until loaves are golden and hollow sounding when tapped.

**Makes 4 mini loaves 6 cm x 12 cm (2½ in x 5 in)**

# GARLIC ROLLS

**250 g (8 oz) plain (baker's/all-purpose) flour**

**2 teaspoons baking powder**

**½ teaspoon salt**

**1 teaspoon sugar**

**90 g (3 oz) butter**

**3 to 4 cloves garlic, finely chopped**

**125 ml (4 fl oz) milk**

**1 egg yolk and 1 tablespoon milk, beaten together, to glaze**

**sesame seeds or poppy seeds, optional**

**1** Preheat oven to 200°C (400°F) and grease a heavy-duty baking tray.

**2** Put flour, baking powder, salt and sugar in a bowl and mix well. Rub in butter until mixture resembles breadcrumbs, then add garlic. Gradually work in milk, mixing until the dough starts to clump. Transfer to a floured surface and knead until a smooth, soft dough forms.

**3** Divide dough into 8 equal portions, then knead each one into a ball. Transfer to prepared baking tray, allowing room for spreading. Press each roll down slightly, then make a cross over the surface of each one using the back of a floured knife. Brush the tops with egg yolk/milk mixture, sprinkle seeds over this then transfer to oven.

**4** Bake for 20 minutes, reduce temperature to 180°C (350°F) and continue to bake until golden, another 10 to 12 minutes. Transfer to wire racks to cool.

**Makes 8 rolls**

*Garlic Rolls; Mini Cheese and Salami Loav*

*Pumpkin and Currant Buns; Cheese and Onion French Stick*

# PUMPKIN AND CURRANT BUNS

**4 tablespoons sugar**

**1 sachet (7 g/¼ oz) active dry yeast**

**60 ml (2 fl oz) + 250 ml (8 fl oz) warm water (41°C to 42°C/106°F to 108°F), comfortable to the fingers**

**1 teaspoon salt**

**60 g (2 oz) butter, softened**

**1 cup mashed cooked pumpkin, thoroughly drained**

**125 g (4 oz) currants**

**1 teaspoon mixed spice**

**625 g (21 oz) plain (baker's/all-purpose) flour**

**1** Put sugar and yeast in a small bowl and stir in ¼ cup (60 ml/2 fl oz) warm water. Set aside for 5 minutes until foaming.

**2** In a large bowl put 1 cup (250 ml/8 fl oz) warm water, salt and butter. Stir until butter has melted. Stir in yeast mixture, then add pumpkin, currants and mixed spice.

**3** Add half the flour and beat well with a wooden spoon. Add enough of the remaining flour to give a soft dough which clumps around the spoon. Transfer to a floured surface and knead until dough is smooth and elastic; 8 to 10 minutes.

**4** Lightly oil a large bowl. Put in dough and roll it around to oil its surface. Cover bowl tightly with plastic wrap or a plastic

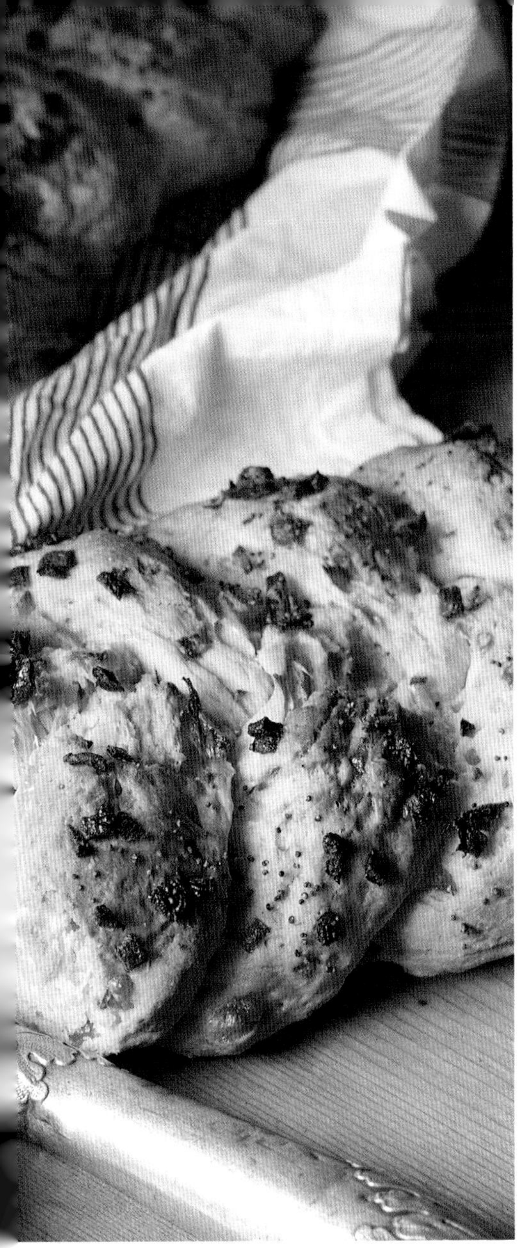

bag and set aside in a protected spot until doubled in size, 1½ to 2 hours. Punch dough down several times to cause it to collapse. (At this stage divide dough into two and freeze half if only 18 buns are required.)

**5** Lightly oil a heavy-based baking dish. Break off portions of dough and roll into 5 cm (2 in) balls. Arrange side by side, but not touching, in prepared dish. Brush tops lightly with oil, slide dish into a plastic bag and set aside in a protected spot until dough has doubled in size again; about 30 minutes.

**6** In the meantime, preheat oven to 220°C (425°F). Transfer buns to oven and bake until golden, about 30 minutes.

**MAKES 36 BUNS**

# CHEESE AND ONION FRENCH STICK

**20 g (½ oz) butter**

**1 tablespoon vegetable oil**

**1 large onion, chopped**

**500 g (16 oz) plain (baker's/all-purpose) flour**

**1½ teaspoons salt**

**4 teaspoons baking powder**

**2 teaspoons dry mustard**

**¼ teaspoon pepper**

**125 g (4 oz) butter, extra**

**125 g (4 oz) shredded cheddar cheese**

**1 egg, lightly beaten**

**300 ml (10 fl oz) milk**

**1 egg beaten with 2 to 3 tablespoons milk, for glazing**

**1½ tablespoons sesame or poppy seeds**

**1** Preheat oven to 220°C (425°F) and grease a heavy-duty baking tray.

**2** Melt butter and oil in a frying pan and cook onion over a low heat for 10 minutes without browning. Transfer to paper towels with a slotted spoon and set aside.

**3** Put flour, salt, baking powder, mustard and pepper in a large bowl and mix well. Rub in butter until mixture resembles fine breadcrumbs. Stir through cheddar then add egg and milk. Stir until mixture clumps around the spoon, then continue mixing by hand until a rough dough forms. Knead on a lightly floured surface until smooth.

**4** Divide dough in half, then divide each half into three. With floured fingers, roll each portion into a long roll of 45 cm (18 in). Press three rolls together at one end then plait together. Join final ends neatly. Make second loaf with remaining three rolls. Transfer plaits to prepared tray, patting them into a neat shape. Brush surfaces with egg/milk mixture, sprinkle with reserved onion and then sesame seeds. Transfer to oven and bake until golden brown and hollow sounding when tapped, about 30 minutes.

**MAKES 2 LOAVES**

**≈ PUMPKIN AND CURRANT BUNS**

*Unusual and slightly sweet, these buns are delicious served warm with butter. The secret is to use very dry mashed pumpkin, one with a strong flavour and hard texture to begin with, not Butternut. If it is baked rather than boiled there will be less liquid, and mash the pulp, don't purée it in a processor.*

**≈ Rice Buns**

*In these buns egg whites are used as well as baking powder to leaven the dough.*

# RICE BUNS

**2 eggs, separated**

**185 g (6 oz) cooked rice (220 g/7 oz raw)**

**2 tablespoons finely chopped parsley**

**1 tablespoon finely chopped chives**

**185 g (6 oz) plain (baker's/all-purpose) flour**

**2 teaspoons baking powder**

**1 teaspoon caster sugar**

**1 teaspoon salt**

**250 ml (8 fl oz) milk**

**1** Preheat oven to 200°C (400°F) and grease 12 moulds or muffin tins.

**2** Beat egg yolks in a bowl then stir in rice, parsley and chives.

**3** Combine flour, baking powder, sugar and salt in a large bowl and mix well. Stir through egg/rice mixture then gradually stir in milk until just combined.

**4** In another bowl beat egg whites with a pinch of salt until they hold stiff peaks. Lightly fold one third of whites through rice mixture, followed by the remaining two thirds. Stop folding as soon as mixture is evenly mixed.

**5** Distribute between prepared tins and transfer to oven. Baked until puffed and golden, about 20 minutes.

**Makes 12 buns**

# HERBED TWISTED ROLLS

**315 g (10 oz) plain (baker's/all-purpose) flour**

**2 teaspoons baking powder**

**½ teaspoon bicarbonate of soda**

**1 teaspoon salt**

**1 egg, lightly beaten**

**1 tablespoon milk**

**250 ml (8 fl oz) buttermilk**

**75 g (2½ oz) butter, melted and cooled**

**1 tablespoon sesame seeds**

**½ tablespoon dry oregano**

**1** Preheat oven to 230°C (450°F) and lightly brush a heavy-duty baking tray with oil.

**2** Put flour, baking powder, bicarbonate of soda and salt into a bowl and mix well. Pour in three quarters of the egg. To the remaining one quarter whisk in 1 tablespoon of milk and reserve for glazing. Add buttermilk and butter to flour and stir until mixture clumps around the spoon. Continue mixing by hand until a dough forms, then knead on a floured surface until smooth, 20 to 30 seconds.

**3** Roll dough into a rope of approximately 5 cm (2 in) diameter. Slice this into 16 equal segments, then roll each of these into a rope 20 cm (8 in) long with tapering ends. Working one at a time, fold each rope in half so that the two halves are touching side by side. Keeping the folded end in position, twist the length twice and press tapered ends together neatly. Arrange twists untouching on prepared tray. Brush surfaces with reserved egg/milk, sprinkle sesame seeds and oregano on top and rest for 10 minutes before transferring to the oven.

**4** Bake until golden, about 15 minutes.

**Makes 16 rolls**

# RICOTTA BREAD

**1 sachet (7 g/¼ oz) active dry yeast**

**60 ml (2 fl oz) warm water, comfortable to the fingers (41°C to 42°C/106°F to 108°F)**

**2 tablespoons sugar**

**1 cup dry ricotta cheese**

**30 g (1 oz) butter, softened**

**1 tablespoon finely minced onion**

**1 teaspoon salt**

**1 teaspoon celery seeds**

**¼ teaspoon bicarbonate of soda**

**1 egg**

**345 g (11 oz) plain (baker's/all-purpose) flour**

1 Stir yeast, water and sugar together in a small bowl and set aside to foam, about 5 minutes.

2 Briefly whisk ricotta in processor until smooth. Add butter, onion, salt, celery seeds, bicarbonate of soda and egg and whisk to combine. Add foaming yeast mixture and 250 g (8 oz) of the flour. Mix until well blended. Gradually add remaining flour until a smooth dough forms. Remove from processor and knead on a floured surface for 6 to 8 minutes. Transfer to an oiled bowl, roll it around a few times to coat surface then cover tightly with plastic wrap or a plastic bag. Set aside in a protected spot until doubled in size, about 1 hour.

3 Knock dough down, shape into a round loaf and place in an oiled 22 cm to 24 cm (8½ in to 9½ in) round casserole dish. Cover and set aside to rise again until doubled, about 30 minutes.

4 In the meantime, preheat oven to 180°C (350°F). When dough has proved, transfer to oven and bake until golden and hollow sounding when tapped, 45 to 50 minutes. Turn out onto a wire rack to cool.

**MAKES 1 ROUND LOAF OF APPROXIMATELY 22 CM (8½ IN)**

*Ricotta Bread served with onion, cheese and salami*

**≈ RICOTTA BREAD**

*Although made with yeast, this bread is so easy to mix in a processor and so unusual that the extra time needed for rising is worth the wait!*

*Little Watercress Loaves*

# LITTLE WATERCRESS LOAVES

**375 g (12 oz) plain (baker's/all-purpose) flour**

**1 teaspoon salt**

**4½ teaspoons baking powder**

**¼ teaspoon dry mustard**

**¾ cup tightly packed chopped watercress**

**2 spring onions, finely chopped**

**100 g (3½ oz) butter, melted and cooled**

**250 ml (8 fl oz) milk**

**extra milk for glazing**

**1** Preheat oven to 200°C (400°F) and grease 6 mini loaf tins 6 cm x 12 cm x 4 cm (2½ in x 5 in x 1½ in) or use two large loaf tins and separate the loaves with aluminium foil covered dividers as described in Mini Cheese and Salami Loaves (page 56).

**2** In a large bowl put flour, salt, baking powder and mustard and mix well.

**3** Wring watercress out in a clean tea towel or muslin to extract as much moisture as possible. Add to flour along with onions and toss to distribute evenly. Stir in butter and milk and mix until a loose dough forms. Turn out onto a floured surface and knead lightly until smooth, 25 to 30 seconds.

**4** Divide dough into 6 pieces and lightly shape each to fit into tins. Place in tins, brush surfaces with milk and transfer to oven. Bake until golden and hollow sounding when tapped, about 20 minutes. Turn out onto wire racks to cool.

**MAKES 6 LOAVES 6 CM X 12 CM X 4 CM (2½ IN X 5 IN X 1½ IN)**

**≈ LITTLE WATERCRESS LOAVES**

*These may be served warm or cold, sliced or whole, with or without butter. As well as being ideal to serve with a cold luncheon or salads, they complement roast meats and baked fish.*

# SAILOR'S BREAD

**125 g (4 oz) sultanas**

**4 tablespoons fortified wine eg Madeira or sherry**

**250 g (8 oz) plain (baker's/all-purpose) flour**

**2 teaspoons baking powder**

**100 g (3½ oz) mixed candied peel**

**3 teaspoons fennel seeds**

**½ teaspoon ground cumin**

**¼ teaspoon cinnamon**

**180 g (6 oz) butter**

**5 tablespoons sugar**

**2 eggs (1 whole, 1 separated)**

**2 tablespoons milk**

**1 tablespoon milk, extra**

**1** Preheat oven to 180°C (350°F) and grease a baking tray.

**2** Put sultanas and wine in a small bowl and set aside.

**3** Put flour, baking powder, mixed peel, fennel, cumin and cinnamon in a bowl and stir well.

**4** This step may be done in an electric mixer or using a hand held mixer. In a separate bowl, cream butter and sugar until smooth and pale lemon in colour, about 5 minutes. Beat in egg and egg yolk. Gradually beat in half the flour mixture then add milk and sultanas/wine. Continue to add remaining flour until it is all used; a loose dough will clump around the spoon (or around the beaters of an electric mixer).

**5** Transfer dough to a floured surface and continue mixing by hand. It should be soft and damp, but not sticky. Knead lightly until smooth, 2 to 3 minutes. Divide in half and shape each into a ball. Press down on the dough to form a flat circle 3 cm (1¼ in) high.

**6** Transfer loaves to prepared tray. Whisk the egg white and 1 tablespoon of milk together and brush surfaces with the mixture. With a floured knife, make a cross pattern on the surfaces, similar to the cross in noughts and crosses.

**7** Bake loaves in oven until golden and hollow sounding when tapped, about 40 minutes. Cool on wire racks before serving.

**MAKES 2 LOAVES OF 18 CM TO 20 CM (7 IN TO 8 IN) DIAMETER**

# SWEET POTATO BUNS

**155 g (5 oz) plain (baker's/all-purpose) flour**

**1 tablespoon baking powder**

**2 level teaspoons tightly packed brown sugar**

**½ teaspoon salt**

**90 g (3 oz) butter**

**1 egg**

**½ cup cooked and dry mashed sweet potato**

**2 tablespoons milk**

**1** Preheat oven to 220°C (425°F) and lightly dust a baking tray with flour.

**2** Put flour, baking powder, sugar and salt into a bowl and stir well. Cut in butter until mix resembles coarse breadcrumbs. Add egg, sweet potato and milk and stir until dough just starts to cling together. Turn out onto a floured surface and knead lightly and briefly until uniform in texture.

**3** Pat dough to a round 1 cm (½ in) thick. With a 6 cm (2½ in) cookie cutter cut out 8 buns. Position on prepared tray in a circle, barely touching each other. Transfer to oven and bake until golden, 10 to 12 minutes. Serve hot or at room temperature.

**MAKES 8**

**≈ SAILOR'S BREAD**

*This bread has been accredited to history's great bakers, the Mesopotamians. Not so much a reference to any sea-faring skills they may have possessed, but more as a result of their ingenious bread making: producing the right loaf for the right occasion. As sailors explored and fished the Mediterranean a need arose for a nourishing staple food that had good keeping qualities. These loaves, the specialties of coastal towns and fishing villages, are still popular for the same old reasons: quick to make, keep for a week or more and have a good spicy fruit flavour.*

**≈ Black Olive Bread**

*An attractive bread with a good olive flavour, this becomes a good loaf, when it has passed its prime, for making bruschetta. Brush slices lightly with olive oil and fry, grill or toast until golden.*

# BLACK OLIVE BREAD

**250 g (8 oz) plain (baker's/all-purpose) flour**

**1 tablespoon sugar**

**¼ teaspoon salt**

**2 teaspoons baking powder**

**pinch dried oregano**

**150 g (5 oz) sliced pitted black olives**

**3 eggs, lightly beaten**

**125 ml (4 fl oz) milk**

**1** Preheat oven to 190°C (375°F) and grease four 10 cm (4 in) round deep pie dishes or ramekins — sides need to be at least 5 cm (2 in) deep.

**2** Combine flour, sugar, salt, baking powder and oregano in a large bowl and stir with a wooden spoon to blend. Add olives and toss to coat with flour. Beat in eggs and milk and continue mixing until a uniform, slightly sticky batter forms.

**3** Distribute mixture evenly between prepared dishes, smoothing the top with the back of a spoon dipped in olive oil. Tap the dishes hard 3 or 4 times against the kitchen bench to settle mixture then set aside to rest for 15 minutes.

**4** Transfer to oven and bake until golden and hollow sounding when tapped, about 20 minutes.

**5** Turn out immediately onto wire racks to cool.

**Makes four 10 cm (4 in) round loaves or two 7 cm x 16 cm (2¾ in x 6½ in) small oblong loaves**

# GREEN OLIVE AND ALMOND BREAD

**500 g (16 oz) plain (baker's/all-purpose) flour**

**1 teaspoon salt**

**3 teaspoons baking powder**

**1 teaspoon bicarbonate of soda**

**¼ teaspoon cardamom**

**60 g (2 oz) butter**

**60 g (2 oz) blanched almonds, coarsely chopped**

**125 g (4 oz) pitted green olives, sliced**

**1 egg**

**430 ml (13½ fl oz) buttermilk**

**1** Preheat oven to 190°C (375°F) and grease two deep-sided 20 cm (8 in) round cake tins.

**2** Put flour, salt, baking powder, bicarbonate of soda and cardamom in a bowl and mix well. Cut in butter until mix resembles coarse breadcrumbs. Stir through almonds and green olives, then add egg and buttermilk. Stir until mix clumps around the spoon. Turn out onto a floured surface, finish mixing by hand then knead until smooth, 2 to 3 minutes.

**3** Divide dough in half, shape each into a round and place in prepared tins. Press dough down to mould to tins, then cut a cross in the surface of each one. Transfer to oven and bake until golden and hollow sounding when tapped, 30 to 35 minutes. If necessary, switch position of tins halfway through baking time for even baking. Cool on wire racks before serving.

**Makes 2 loaves**

*Green Olive and Almond Bread; Walnut and Potato Bread*

# WALNUT AND POTATO BREAD

**200 g (6½ oz) walnut halves**

**250 g (8 oz) plain (baker's/all-purpose) flour**

**2½ teaspoons baking powder**

**150 g (5 oz) grated parmesan cheese**

**3 tablespoons chopped mint**

**400 g (13 oz) cooked potatoes, cut into 1 cm (½ in) cubes**

**8 eggs, lightly beaten**

**150 g (5 oz) butter, melted and slightly cooled**

**4 tablespoons grated cheddar cheese**

Preheat oven to 190°C (375°F) and grease two 8 cm x 26 cm (3 in x 10½ in) loaf tins.

**2** Put walnuts in a small bowl and cover with water. Soak for 10 minutes, then drain. Spread on a baking tray and crisp in the preheating oven for 5 minutes.

**3** Put flour, baking powder, parmesan, mint, potatoes and walnuts in a bowl and mix well. Add eggs and butter and stir in. Divide mixture between prepared tins, smooth the tops and transfer to oven.

**4** Bake for 15 minutes, then scatter cheddar over the tops. Return to oven until golden and hollow sounding when tapped, another 15 to 20 minutes.

**MAKES TWO 8 CM X 26 CM (3 IN X 10½ IN) LOAVES**

# FLATBREADS

Flatbreads are the simplest and the most primitive of breads. They originated with the hearthbreads of open fire cooking, when a heated flat stone was the only utensil needed and ingredients were basic and few.

They have changed little over the centuries and the invention of the oven and the discovery of yeast are the main concessions to modernity in all that time. It is ironic that these breads, with the humblest of origins, are currently regarded as chic.

*Spring Onion Flatbread (page 68); Rich Focaccia with Prosciutto (page 69); Rosemary, Onion and Olive Schiacciata (page 68)*

**≈ Rosemary, Onion and Olive Schiacciata**

*In the Italian regions of Tuscany and Umbria flat hearthbreads are called schiacciata. They were originally introduced into the northern regions of Italy by the Etruscans and were cooked on heated flat stones, schiacce. Now they are usually baked and, having gone through a stage where they were quite large slabs of bread, are popular today as smaller discs to be nibbled on as a snack. Traditionally made with a yeast dough, they adapt well to other doughs which take no time at all to prepare.*

# ROSEMARY, ONION AND OLIVE SCHIACCIATA

**250 g (8 oz) plain (baker's/all-purpose) flour**

**2½ teaspoons salt**

**½ teaspoon bicarbonate of soda**

**180 ml (6 fl oz) buttermilk**

**1 medium onion, thinly sliced**

**extra virgin olive oil**

**1 tablespoon roughly chopped fresh rosemary leaves**

**50 g (2 oz) seeded and sliced black olives**

**1** This step may be done in a processor. Put flour, ½ teaspoon salt and bicarbonate of soda into a bowl and mix well. Gradually stir in buttermilk and when mixture begins to clump, transfer to a floured surface. Knead until uniform and smooth. Cover with a tea towel or plastic bag and rest for 20 minutes before use.

**2** Preheat oven to 200°C (400°F) and brush a baking tray with oil.

**3** In a small bowl toss onion with remaining 2 teaspoons salt and set aside 10 minutes.

**4** Roll out and shape dough into a circle of 25 cm (10 in) diameter and transfer to prepared tray. Brush surface with extra virgin olive oil. Drain off and discard liquid from onions then scatter them over dough. Sprinkle on rosemary, followed by the olives. Drizzle over a little more extra virgin olive oil.

**5** Transfer to oven and bake until golden, 20 to 25 minutes. Serve warm or at room temperature.

**Makes one 25 cm (10 in) circle**

# SPRING ONION FLATBREAD

**1 teaspoon vegetable oil**

**½ cm (¼ in) piece peeled fresh ginger, finely minced**

**½ clove garlic, minced**

**185 g (6 oz) spring onions (green onions), some green included, finely sliced**

**220 g (7 oz) plain (baker's/all-purpose) flour**

**1 teaspoon salt**

**250 ml (8 fl oz) boiling water**

**vegetable oil for frying**

**1** Heat 1 teaspoon of oil in a pan and gently sauté ginger, garlic and onion until softened, about 5 minutes.

**2** In a bowl combine flour and salt. Add onion mixture and stir to coat. Gradually stir in water until a loose dough forms then continue mixing with floured hands to give a smooth dough. Knead for 1½ to 2 minutes. Cover with plastic wrap and rest for 30 minutes.

**3** Divide dough into 12 equal parts. Roll each one out on a floured surface to a thin circle of 15 cm (6 in) diameter.

**4** Fill a frying pan with oil to a depth of 2 cm (¾ in) and place over a moderately hot flame. When oil begins to shimmer, test by dropping in a small piece of dough. When this dances on the surface, the oil is ready. Working one at a time, fry breads until crisp and golden, 25 to 30 seconds each side. Drain well on absorbent paper and allow to cool before serving.

**Makes 12 flatbreads**

# RICH FOCACCIA WITH PROSCIUTTO

**250 g (8 oz) plain (baker's/all-purpose) flour**

**½ teaspoon salt**

**½ teaspoon bicarbonate of soda**

**20 (½ oz) butter**

**1 tablespoon olive oil**

**1 egg, lightly beaten**

**125 ml (4 fl oz) buttermilk**

**50 g (2 oz) parmesan cheese, grated**

**50 g (2 oz) provolone or gouda cheese, shredded**

**80 g (2½ oz) lean prosciutto or bacon, cut into very fine dice**

**extra virgin olive oil**

**1** Put flour, salt and bicarbonate of soda into a bowl and mix well. Rub in butter, then add olive oil, egg and buttermilk. Stir until mixture begins to unite, then add all of the parmesan, three quarters of the provolone and prosciutto. Mix to form a loose dough. Turn out onto a floured surface and begin kneading. It may be necessary to add a little more flour or olive oil to maintain a soft but non-sticky texture. Knead until uniform and smooth, no more than 3 minutes. Cover with a tea towel or plastic bag and set aside to rest for 20 minutes.

**2** In the meantime, preheat oven to 200°C (400°F) and grease a pizza or baking tray.

**3** Put dough in the centre of prepared tray and press with the heel of the hand. Working from the middle towards the outside, press and flatten dough to a circle approximately 25 cm (10 in) diameter. Brush the surface with extra virgin olive oil and scatter remaining provolone on top. Rest, uncovered, for 10 minutes.

**4** Transfer to oven and bake for 15 minutes, then reduce temperature to 180°C (350°F) and continue baking until golden.

**MAKES ONE 25 CM (10 IN) FOCACCIA**

# CORNBREAD WITH GREEN OLIVES

**185 g (6 oz) plain (baker's/all-purpose) flour**

**85 g (3 oz) fine cornmeal (polenta)**

**½ teaspoon salt**

**½ teaspoon bicarbonate of soda**

**20 g (½ oz) butter, melted**

**180 ml (6 fl oz) buttermilk**

**15 green olives, pitted and halved**

**olive oil for brushing**

**ground coarse sea salt or Maldon sea salt**

**1** Preheat oven to 200°C (400°F) and brush a pizza or baking tray with oil.

**2** This step may be done in a processor. Put flour, cornmeal, salt and bicarbonate of soda in a bowl and mix well. Stir in butter and buttermilk and continue mixing until a loose dough forms.

**3** Transfer to a floured surface and knead until smooth, 1 minute. Form into a ball then squash it out by pressing down on the centre. Starting from the middle and working out, press dough into a flat circle 1 cm (½ in) thick. Don't try for a smooth, even surface.

**4** Transfer to prepared tray. Distribute olives over the top, pressing them in gently to stick. Lightly brush surface with olive oil then sprinkle on salt. Rest for 20 minutes before baking. Place bread in the oven and bake. The bread is done when it is golden with a slightly crisp crust, approximately 20 minutes.

**MAKES 1 BREAD OF APPROXIMATELY 26 CM (10½ IN) DIAMETER**

*Potato Focaccia*

**≈ Potato Focaccia**
*Here is a focaccia with a difference: no flour and no leavening agent. To us, it is a potato pie, but to its devotees in Apulia in southern Italy, definitely a focaccia!*

# POTATO FOCACCIA

**500 g (16 oz) potatoes**
**3 eggs**
**3 tablespoons dry white wine**
**90 g (3 oz) good quality parmesan cheese, grated**
**freshly ground black pepper**
**100 g (3½ oz) bacon or ham, cut into small pieces**
**1 tablespoon finely chopped parsley**

**1** Preheat oven to 180°C (350°F) and grease a round cake tin of 25 cm (10 in) diameter and a 2.5 cm (1 in) depth.

**2** Peel then grate potatoes into a bowl of cold water to prevent discolouration.

**3** Beat eggs, wine and parmesan together in a large bowl and season to taste with black pepper.

**4** Wring potatoes dry in a tea towel or muslin and add to egg mixture along with bacon and parsley. Stir to evenly distribute. Transfer to prepared tin and bake until potatoes are cooked and the crust is golden, 45 to 55 minutes. If the edges appear to be browning prematurely, reduce temperature to 160°C (320°F). Serve cut into wedges straight from the oven, or bring to room temperature and cut into smaller slices to use as you would more traditional bread.

**Makes 1 loaf of 25 cm (10 in) diameter**

*Pepper and Poppy Seed Crispbreads (page 72); Parmesan Flatbread (page 72)*

**≈ Pepper and Poppy Seed Crispbreads**

*This method of making a quick, ready-in-minutes bread has been around for thousands of years and is still common, particularly in the Middle East and North Africa. The breads puff up when cooked and so are designed for immediate consumption; it is the dough (or at least the ingredients) which is transportable, not the finished product. For the busy cook in a modern kitchen, the breads can be prepared up to the point of frying, separated with plastic wrap or greaseproof paper then popped in a plastic bag and refrigerated until needed, up to 24 hours.*

# PEPPER AND POPPY SEED CRISPBREADS

**125 g (4 oz) plain (baker's/all-purpose) flour**

**155 g (5 oz) wholemeal flour**

**1 teaspoon salt**

**½ teaspoon cayenne pepper (or to taste)**

**2 tablespoons vegetable oil**

**approximately 160 ml (5 fl oz) warm water**

**2 to 3 tablespoons poppy seeds**

**vegetable oil for frying**

**1** Put flours, salt and cayenne into a bowl and mix well. Add oil and half the water, mix, then gradually add remaining water until a loose dough forms which clumps around the spoon. This step may be done up to this stage in a processor. Transfer dough to a floured surface and knead until smooth and elastic, about 6 minutes. Cover and rest at room temperature for 20 minutes.

**2** Divide dough in half and roll each into a 20 cm (8 in) thick cylinder. Cut each one into 12 equal sections. Flatten each of these between the hands first, then roll them out very thinly. Just before the final roll on each side, sprinkle some poppy seeds over the surface then roll them in. Keep the rolled breads covered as you work.

**3** Fill a deep frying pan with oil to a depth of 5 cm to 6 cm (2 in to 2½ in) and place over a high heat. When the oil begins to shimmer, drop in a small piece of dough. If it dances on the surface, the oil is hot enough. Working one at a time, drop bread into oil. Keep it submerged with a metal spatula or egg slice for 8 to 10 seconds, then turn over and cook the other side for a few seconds more. They will turn golden and puff up. Drain on paper towels and serve immediately.

**Makes 24 crispbreads**

# PARMESAN FLATBREAD

**375 g (12 oz) plain (baker's/all-purpose) flour**

**90 g (3 oz) good quality parmesan cheese, grated**

**1 teaspoon salt**

**2 teaspoons baking powder**

**50 g (2 oz) butter, melted**

**2 eggs**

**200 ml (6½ fl oz) milk**

**1 teaspoon dried or chopped fresh sage**

**1** Preheat oven to 190°C (375°F) and brush a baking tray with oil.

**2** This step may be done in a processor. Put flour, cheese, salt and baking powder in a bowl and stir well. Add butter, eggs and milk and stir until mixture begins to clump around the spoon. Transfer to a floured surface and finish mixing by hand. When a soft but not sticky dough forms knead lightly for 1½ to 2 minutes.

**3** Form into a ball then transfer to prepared tray. Working outward from the centre, press dough to flatten it out to an oblong 1 cm (½ in) thick; it will be approximately 22 cm x 30 cm (8¾ in x 12 in). Sprinkle sage over the top then set aside to rest for 20 minutes. Bake in oven until golden, about 20 minutes.

**Makes 1 bread 22 cm x 30 cm (8¾ in x 12 in)**

# HEARTHBREAD WITH BLACK PEPPER AND SAGE

**250 g (8 oz) plain (baker's/all-purpose) flour**
**½ teaspoon baking powder**
**½ tablespoon caster sugar**
**½ teaspoon salt**
**1 egg**
**100 ml (3½ fl oz) olive oil**
**50 ml (2 fl oz) dry white wine**
**freshly ground black pepper, to taste**
**15 small fresh sage leaves, finely chopped**
**extra olive oil for brushing**

**1** This step may be done in a processor. Put flour, baking powder, caster sugar and salt in a bowl and mix well. Add egg, olive oil and wine and stir until mixture clumps together.

**2** Toss pepper and sage leaves together in a little bowl.

**3** Briefly knead dough on a floured surface and as it becomes smoother, add pepper/sage mix. Knead for 2 to 3 minutes then cover with a plastic bag and set aside to rest for 20 minutes.

**4** In the meantime, preheat oven to 220°C (425°F) and lightly brush a heavy-duty baking tray with oil.

**5** Divide dough in two. Working one half at a time, form into flat circles by pressing in the centre and moving out to the edges. Stop when they are of 20 cm to 22 cm (8 in to 8¾ in) diameter. Position on prepared tray, lightly brush tops with olive oil and set aside to rest for 10 minutes. Transfer to oven and bake until golden and the crust is slightly crisp, about 15 minutes.

**MAKES 2 BREADS OF 20 CM (8 IN) DIAMETER**

# SPICED WHOLEMEAL FLATBREAD

**200 g (6½ oz) wholemeal flour**
**½ teaspoon salt**
**½ teaspoon cayenne pepper**
**¼ teaspoon ground cumin**
**pinch ground cloves**
**150 ml (5 fl oz) water**
**100 ml (3½ fl oz) milk**
**100 g (3½ oz) melted butter or ghee, + extra for frying.**

**1** Put flour, salt, cayenne, cumin and cloves in a bowl and mix well. Pour in water and milk and stir to combine. The dough will be very soft, but not unmanageable. Transfer to a floured surface and knead until smooth, adding as little flour as possible. Cover with a damp tea towel or a plastic bag and rest for at least 2 hours, or overnight.

**2** Divide dough into 6 equal pieces. Working one at a time, roll each out to a circle of approximately 18 cm (7 in) diameter. Brush with melted butter then fold in half to form a half moon shape. Fold in half again, forming a triangle. Roll out again to original size, brush with butter and repeat folding. Continue to roll, butter and fold at least 6 times more, finishing with thin 18 cm (7 in) circles.

**3** Heat a griddle or heavy-based iron frying pan. Brush lightly with butter and fry breads on both sides, buttering as you go, until mottled golden brown and cooked through. Serve at once.

**MAKES SIX 18 CM (7 IN) FLATBREADS**

**≈ SPICED WHOLEMEAL FLATBREAD**

*This style of flatbread is used all around the Mediterranean and in the Middle and Far East as a means of eating dishes without utensils. Pita and Arab bread, the Italian piadina and even the paratha in India are examples. Either pieces are broken off and used to scoop up cooked vegetables and meats, or the bread is used as a casing to wrap around a filling. The texture needs to be soft and pliable, yet strong enough to support other ingredients without tearing.*

# FLATBREAD WITH WALNUTS

**60 g (2 oz) walnut halves**

**250 g (8 oz) plain (baker's/all-purpose) flour**

**pinch salt**

**250 g (8 oz) butter, cut into small pieces**

**2 eggs, lightly beaten**

**125 ml (4 fl oz) cream**

**1 egg yolk, beaten**

**1** Soak walnuts in water to cover for 30 minutes.

**2** In the meantime, mix flour and salt in a bowl. Rub in butter, then add eggs and cream. Stir with a spoon until mixture begins to clump, then continue mixing by hand. When a loose dough is formed, knead lightly until smooth. Rest, covered, for 30 minutes.

**3** Preheat oven to 220°C (425°F) and grease a heavy-based baking tray.

**4** On a floured surface, roll out dough to a circle of approximately 25 cm (10 in). Fold over once to form a half moon shape, then once again to form a triangle. Roll out to original size then repeat folding. Do this three times in all, ending with a triangle shape. Rest, covered, for 10 minutes. Roll out to a thickness of 1.5 cm (¾ in) and transfer to prepared tray. Brush surface with egg yolk.

**5** Drain walnuts and pat dry, sprinkle over surface of bread and lightly press them in. With the back of a knife, cut a noughts and crosses type cross on top. Transfer to oven and bake until golden; about 30 minutes.

**MAKES ONE BREAD OF APPROXIMATELY 25 CM (10 IN) DIAMETER**

# CRISPBREADS FROM MALTA

**4 anchovy fillets, drained and chopped**

**2 tablespoons milk**

**500 g (16 oz) plain (baker's/all-purpose) flour**

**1 teaspoon salt**

**1 teaspoon baking powder**

**½ onion, chopped finely**

**½ red capsicum (pepper), chopped finely**

**extra 100 ml (3½ fl oz) milk**

**100 ml (3½ fl oz) water**

**approx 60 g (2 oz) butter, melted**

**1** In a small bowl soak anchovies in milk for 15 minutes.

**2** Put flour, salt and baking powder in a bowl and mix well. Add onion and red capsicum (pepper) and toss to combine. Add anchovies with their milk, extra milk and water and stir until mixture clumps around the spoon. Continue mixing by hand, then knead until smooth. Place in a plastic bag and rest for at least 1 hour.

**3** Preheat oven to 200°C (400°F).

**4** Break off pieces of dough the size of a ping-pong ball and shape into a ball. You will have 15 to 18 balls. Roll each one out on a floured surface to a flat disc 3 mm (⅛ in) thick. Working a few at a time, brush both sides with melted butter and position on a heavy-based baking tray, untouching.

**5** Transfer to oven and bake until underside is crisp and golden, about 5 minutes, then turn breads over for an extra 3 to 4 minutes to brown both sides evenly. Remove from oven and allow to cool before serving. The cooler they get, the crisper they become.

**MAKES 15 TO 18 CRISPBREADS**

*Crispbreads from Malta; Flatbread with Walnuts*

**≈ Focaccia with Salt and Olive Oil**

*Named from 'focus', the Latin for hearth, focaccia were baked by housewives on heated hearth stones before the oven became commonplace. They originated in Liguria and have always been flavoured simply but with a good combination of flavours and with ingredients of the best quality.*

*This is a traditional recipe made with yeast as it is hard to duplicate the texture and flavour with a yeastless dough and the size of the loaf requires a strong, elastic dough.*

# FOCACCIA WITH SALT AND OLIVE OIL

**1 sachet (7 g/¼ oz) active dry yeast**

**1 teaspoon sugar**

**60 ml (2 fl oz) warm water,comfortable to the fingers (41°C to 42°C/106°F to 108°F)**

**1 kg (2 lb) plain (baker's/all-purpose) flour**

**1 tablespoon salt**

**5 tablespoons olive oil**

**extra 750 ml (24 fl oz) warm water (temperature as above)**

**2 teaspoons coarse sea salt**

**1 sprig fresh rosemary, optional**

**1** In a small bowl stir yeast and sugar into 60 ml (2 fl oz) water and set aside in a protected spot to activate and foam 5 to 8 minutes.

**2** Put flour and salt in a large bowl and mix well. Add 2 tablespoons olive oil, the yeast/sugar mix and extra water. Stir with a wooden spoon until mixture holds together and clumps around spoon. Turn out onto a floured surface and knead until smooth or until a finger impression springs back out, at least 8 minutes. (The dough may be mixed in a heavy-duty processor and kneaded in an electric mixer with a dough hook attachment.) Place dough in a bowl which has been lightly oiled and roll it around to coat surface. Seal bowl well with plastic wrap or slide into a plastic bag and close off opening. Place in a protected spot until doubled in size, about 1½ hours.

**3** Knock dough down and divide in two. Shape each half into a large rectangle approximately 28 cm x 38 cm (11 in x 15 in) and transfer to lightly floured heavy-duty baking trays or large trays with shallow sides. Slip trays into plastic bags or cover with dry tea towels and let sit 30 minutes.

**4** Using your fingertips, dimple surface of dough with impressions as deep as 1 cm (½ in). Again cover trays and set aside in a protected spot for 2 hours, or until dough has doubled. Drizzle remaining 3 tablespoons olive oil over surface, letting it pool in the indentations. Sprinkle over coarse salt and crumbled rosemary leaves.

**5** In the meantime, preheat oven to 200°C (400°F). Transfer focaccia to oven and bake for 20 to 25 minutes, or until golden. Immediately transfer to wire racks to cool, turned upside down to keep crusts crisp. Serve warm or at room temperature, preferably on the same day.

**Makes 2 focaccia 28 cm x 38 cm (11 in x 15 in)**

# GORGONZOLA AND BASIL FOCACCIA

**1 x recipe focaccia dough (see recipe for Focaccia with Salt and Olive Oil this page), omitting salt and rosemary**

**220 g (7 oz) gorgonzola cheese or other creamy blue vein**

**80 ml (2½ fl oz) thick or double cream**

**4 tablespoons chopped walnuts**

**2 teaspoons chopped basil leaves**

**1** Prepare focaccia up to step 4 (see recipe for Focaccia with Salt and Olive Oil this page).

**2** Combine gorgonzola, cream and walnuts in a bowl.

**3** Dimple dough surfaces, then spread cheese mixture over the top. Drizzle over a little olive oil then sprinkle on basil. Proceed as for Focaccia with Salt and Olive Oil, omitting salt and rosemary.

**Makes 2 focaccia 28 cm x 38 cm (11 in x 15 in)**

# CRETAN BREAD

*This is a variation on a cheese bread popular in Crete.*

**250 g (8 oz) (baker's/all-purpose) flour**

**½ teaspoon salt**

**½ teaspoon bicarbonate of soda**

**1 tablespoon sesame oil**

**170 ml (6 fl oz) buttermilk**

**2 eggs**

**60 g (2 oz) kasseri or pecorino cheese, grated**

**60 g (2 oz) coarsely chopped pistachio kernels**

**4 tablespoons sesame seeds**

**2 teaspoons anise or fennel seeds**

**½ teaspoon ground ginger**

**1** Put flour, salt and bicarbonate of soda in a bowl and mix well. Add sesame oil and buttermilk and stir until mix starts to clump around the spoon. Turn out onto a floured surface and finish mixing by hand. Knead until smooth and spongy. Cover and rest at room temperature for 30 minutes.
**2** Preheat oven to 220°C (425°F) and grease a heavy-duty baking tray.
**3** Combine eggs, cheese, pistachio kernels, sesame and anise seeds and ginger in a bowl.
**4** On a floured surface, shape dough to a rectangle approximately 12 cm x 20 cm (5 in x 8 in) and with a slightly raised rim. Spread with egg/cheese mixture. Transfer to oven and bake 5 minutes, then reduce heat to 200°C (400°F). Continue baking until bread is golden and topping browned, another 15 to 20 minutes. Allow to cool before cutting into sections.

**MAKES ONE LOAF 12 CM X 20 CM (5 IN X 8 IN)**

# OLIVE AND PINE NUT FOCACCIA

**1 x recipe focaccia dough (see recipe for Focaccia with Salt and Olive Oil page 76), omitting salt and rosemary**

**225 g (7 oz) olives, mixture of black and green, seeded**

**4 tablespoons pine nuts**

**1** Prepare focaccia up to step 4 (see recipe for Focaccia with Salt and Olive Oil page 76). After dimpling the surface, stud with olives and sprinkle on pine nuts. Continue as for Focaccia with Salt and Olive Oil, but omit salt and rosemary.

**MAKES 2 FOCACCIA 28 CM X 38 CM (11 IN X 15 IN)**

# SCHIACCIATA WITH RICOTTA AND ARTICHOKES

**1 x recipe Buttermilk Dough, (see recipe page 84)**

**100 g (3½ oz) ricotta cheese**

**4 egg yolks**

**2 tablespoons grated parmesan cheese**

**salt and freshly ground black pepper**

**8 artichoke hearts marinated in oil, each cut into 4 slices lengthwise**

**2 tablespoons grated parmesan, extra**

**1 tablespoon finely chopped parsley**

**1** Preheat oven to 220°C (425°F) and brush two baking trays with oil.
**2** Divide dough into quarters and roll or shape each to a circle of 15 cm (6 in) diameter. Position on prepared trays.
**3** In a bowl blend ricotta, egg yolks, parmesan, and salt and pepper lightly. Spread mixture over dough bases then arrange artichoke slices on top. Sprinkle over extra parmesan and parsley. Transfer to oven, reduce temperature to 200°C (400°F) and bake until golden, approximately 20 minutes.

**MAKES FOUR 15 CM (6 IN) SCHIACCIATA**

**≈ SCHIACCIATA WITH RICOTTA AND ARTICHOKES**

*These flatbreads, named from the word schiacciare, to crush or flatten, are to Tuscany and Umbria in Italy what the foccacia is to their neighbouring regions. They too were originally baked on heated flat stones called schiacce, and although quite a large bread was produced, the advent of the oven made a more substantial loaf possible.*

# HARVEST SCHIACCIATA

**350 g (11½ oz) small seedless black grapes**

**2 x recipe Buttermilk Dough, (see recipe page 84)**

**4 tablespoons sugar**

**3 to 4 small sprigs fresh rosemary, optional**

**1** Preheat oven to 120°C (250°F).

**2** Wash grapes, shake off excess water then put in a single layer in a glass or ceramic ovenproof dish. Bake for 10 to 12 minutes, or until sticky but still holding their shape. Remove from oven and increase temperature to 200°C (400°F).

**3** Divide dough in half and roll each out on a floured surface to a 25 cm (10 in) circle approximately 5 mm (¼ in) thick. Brush a baking tray with oil and sprinkle with a little flour. Place 1 circle of dough in the centre and scatter over half the grapes. Lightly press them in then sprinkle on 1 tablespoon of sugar. Cover with remaining dough, matching up edges. Gently press down to make sure that dough is sticking to dough wherever possible. Distribute remaining grapes over the surface, again gently press them in, then sprinkle with remaining sugar. Place rosemary on top. Rest for 10 minutes before transferring to oven.

**4** Bake until golden, 25 to 30 minutes. Allow to cool for 5 to 10 minutes before serving, and remove rosemary sprigs (which will have done the job of imparting a subtle aroma and flavour).

**MAKES ONE 25 CM (10 IN) LOAF**

# PIADINA WITH SALAMI, SUN-DRIED TOMATOES AND BEL PAESE

**DOUGH**

**430 g (13½ oz) plain (baker's/all-purpose) flour**

**1 teaspoon salt**

**2 teaspoons baking powder**

**80 g (2½ oz) butter, melted**

**150 ml (5 fl oz) milk**

**125 ml (4 fl oz) water**

**FILLING**

**24 slices salami**

**4 sun-dried tomatoes in oil, drained and quartered**

**100 g (3½ oz) bel paese cheese (or cheese of choice), sliced thinly**

**1** This step may be done in a processor. Put flour, salt and baking powder in a bowl and mix well. Add butter, milk and water. Blend with a spoon or fork until mix begins to clump, then turn out onto a floured surface and finish mixing by hand. Knead until smooth and soft.

**2** Divide into 8 equal balls and rest for 30 minutes, covered with a tea towel. Roll each out on a floured surface to a circle 3 mm (⅛ in) thick and prick each 5 to 6 times with a fork.

**3** Heat a griddle or heavy-based frying pan. Begin cooking piadini, one at a time, until uniformly scorched golden brown on both sides. They are better slightly underdone rather than crisp and brittle. Cool on racks.

**4** Divide salami slices between breads, add a couple of pieces of sun-dried tomato and cover with slices of cheese. Fold bread over to encase filling and eat as you would a sandwich.

**MAKES EIGHT 8 CM (3 IN) PIADINI**

**≈ PIADINA WITH SALAMI, SUN-DRIED TOMATOES AND BEL PAESE**

*Piadini are unleavened flatbread from the region around Bologna in central northern Italy. First cousins to pita and Arab bread, they are eaten cut into quarters or wrapped around a simple filling.*

*Harvest Schiacciata*

**≈ Cornmeal Flatbread**

*Made with fine cornmeal or polenta, this golden bread is traditionally served with a warm salad of greens, or with tomatoes, extra virgin olive oil and balsamic vinegar. If you have any leftovers, they can be broken into small pieces, fried with oil and garlic and used as croutons to flavour most warm salads.*

# CORNMEAL FLATBREAD

**250g (8 oz) fine cornmeal or polenta**

**125 g (4 oz) plain (baker's/all-purpose) flour**

**½ teaspoon salt**

**freshly ground black pepper**

**3 tablespoons olive oil**

**100 ml (3½ fl oz) hot water**

**100 ml (3½ fl oz) hot milk**

**4 to 5 small sprigs fresh basil**

**1** Preheat oven to 200°C (400°F) and brush a pizza or baking tray with oil.

**2** Put cornmeal, flour and salt in a bowl with one or two twists of the black pepper mill; mix well. Combine 2 tablespoons olive oil with the hot water then add to dry ingredients along with milk. Mix with a fork until a soft paste-like dough forms. Transfer to prepared tray and press into a flat circle 1 cm (½ in) thick and approximately 30 cm (12 in) across. Prick surface 8 to 10 times with a fork, drizzle on remaining 1 tablespoon of oil and lightly press basil into the surface at intervals.

**3** Transfer to oven and bake until golden, approximately 20 minutes. Remove basil from loaf and serve hot.

**Makes 1 bread of approximately 30 cm (12 in) diameter**

# FLATBREAD WITH THREE ONIONS

**1 medium red onion, thinly sliced into rings**

**2 small sweet white onions, thinly sliced into rings**

**1 to 2 tablespoons salt**

**1 x recipe Buttermilk Dough, (see recipe page 84)**

**2 to 3 spring onions (green onions), including some green, chopped**

**8 to 10 fresh oregano leaves**

**extra virgin olive oil**

**1** Preheat oven to 200°C (400°F) and brush a baking tray with oil.

**2** Put red and white onion slices in a bowl and sprinkle generously with salt. Set aside 15 to 20 minutes to draw out liquid. Discard juices and squeeze onions dry.

**3** Roll out and shape dough on a floured surface to a 26 cm (10½ in) circle. Transfer to prepared tray. Distribute onion rings over the surface and sprinkle on spring onions (green onions), pressing them gently into the dough. Arrange oregano on top, then drizzle on oil, making sure that the dough rim is well coated. Transfer to oven and bake until golden, about 20 minutes. Serve at once, or when cooled to room temperature.

**Makes one 26 cm (10½ in) bread**

# SCHIACCIATA IN LAYERS

**1 x recipe Yeastless Pizza Dough, (see recipe page 11)**

**olive oil for brushing**

**2 tablespoons olive oil**

**2 medium onions, sliced**

**50 g (2 oz) spicy Italian sausage**

**18 pitted black olives**

**1 tablespoon capers**

**1 tablespoon finely chopped parsley**

**1** Preheat oven to 240°C (465°F) and brush a pizza or baking tray with oil.

**2** Divide dough in two parts, one slightly larger than the other. Roll out or shape the larger on a floured surface to a 30 cm (12 in) circle. Transfer to prepared tray and brush with oil. Roll out the second piece of dough to a circle of the same thickness. Cover this half and set aside.

**3** Heat oil in a frying pan and gently sauté onion 5 minutes. Remove meat from sausage casing and add to onion. Cook, stirring often, for 10 minutes. Remove from heat and drain off excess oil.

**4** Put onion/sausage mix, olives and capers on a board and chop with a large knife or mezzaluna to a uniform small-grained pulp; don't over chop to a purée. Stir in parsley.

**5** Spread filling over base to within 1.5 cm (¾ in) of the edge. Cover with second dough circle to form a lid. Fold exposed edge of lower circle over and onto the lid. Press to seal, creating a pattern as you work around the edge. Brush top with olive oil and prick 6 to 8 times with a fork. Transfer to oven and bake for 10 minutes. Reduce temperature to 200°C (400°F) and continue baking until golden; another 8 to 10 minutes. Remove from oven and brush surface with olive oil before serving.

**MAKES ONE 30 CM (12 IN) SCHIACCIATA**

# BAKED BREAD SLICES WITH TOMATOES AND ONION

**3 tablespoons olive oil**

**1 medium onion, finely chopped**

**2 garlic cloves, minced**

**1 x tin (440 g/14 oz) peeled tomatoes, drained and chopped**

**¼ teaspoon dried basil, or 3 to 4 fresh leaves, chopped**

**salt and freshly ground black pepper**

**4 to 6 thick slices day-old Italian bread**

**350 ml (11½ fl oz) milk**

**450 g (14½ oz) mozzarella cheese, thinly sliced**

**1** Preheat oven to 200°C (400°F) and grease an 18 cm x 26 cm (7 in x 10½ in) ovenproof baking dish.

**2** Heat oil in a frying pan and gently sauté onion for 5 minutes. Add garlic, tomatoes and basil and cook, stirring from time to time, until thick, about 15 minutes. Season with salt and pepper.

**3** In the meantime, soak bread in milk until moistened right through but not soggy. Transfer to prepared dish in a single layer but squashed closely together. Spread tomato/onion mixture over the surface, then arrange cheese slices on top. Transfer to oven and bake until cheese is crusty, approximately 15 minutes. Cool slightly before cutting into squares.

**SERVES 4 TO 6**

**≈ BAKED BREAD SLICES WITH TOMATOES AND ONION**

*This dish falls somewhere between a pizza and a large baked open sandwich. It is a marvellous way to use up stale bread, and of course any selection of toppings can be used.*

# Filled Breads

Filled breads are most appealing. They are sustaining, good looking and have that element of surprise when the contents are revealed.

They can be small bite-sized turnovers ideal to take on a picnic, or large voluptuous parcels big enough to satisfy a hungry family.

They can be very elegant with a filling of special ingredients, or merely functional as a means of presenting small leftover amounts of cheese, vegetables or meat.

Although the basic dough recipes are yeastless, a yeast dough may be substituted. As well, ready-made short crust pastry could be used at a push for some of the smaller turnovers.

Feel free to vary the sizes, with the proviso that if going from a small parcel to a large one, the dough will need to be rolled a little thicker to support the weight of the filling. Turnovers containing a filling with quite a bit of liquid should be eaten hot, as they will go soggy when cooled.

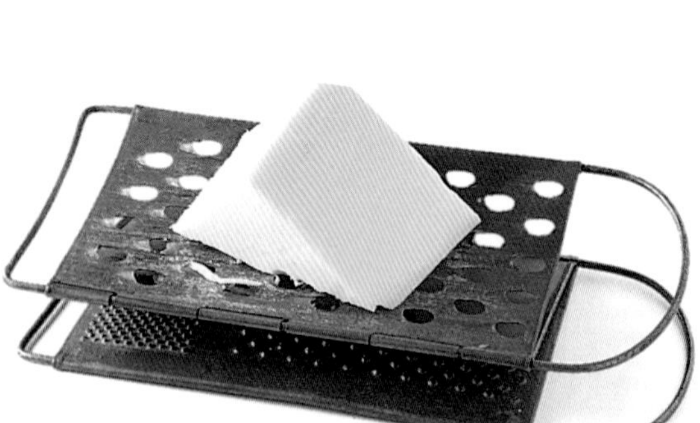

*Prawn (Shrimp) and Fennel Calzoni (page 85); Avocado, Smoked Mozzarella and Tomato Calzone (page 85)*

# BASE RECIPES

**≈ Olive Oil and White Wine Dough**

*With a good texture and a slightly 'fermented' flavour, this dough works well for smaller filled breads. It doesn't rise as much as the buttermilk dough and so gives a thinner, more delicate crust.*

*It is the best recipe to use if the breads are to be fried.*

**≈ Buttermilk Dough**

*This dough gives a strong bread, ideal for supporting large turnovers. It has an appealing, fresh yoghurty taste which matures with age; it starts to resemble sourdough in flavour if left for more than 24 hours.*

## OLIVE OIL AND WHITE WINE DOUGH

**250 g (8 oz) plain (baker's/all-purpose) flour**
**½ teaspoon baking powder**
**½ tablespoon caster sugar**
**½ teaspoon salt**
**1 egg, lightly beaten**
**100 ml (3½ fl oz) olive oil**
**50 ml (2 fl oz) dry white wine**

**1** This step may be done in a processor. Combine flour, baking powder, sugar and salt in a bowl. Gradually mix in egg, oil and wine and when the dough begins to clump, transfer to a floured surface.

**2** Finish mixing by hand, then knead for 3 to 4 minutes until smooth and elastic. Cover and set aside to rest at room temperature for at least 30 minutes before use.

**Makes 1 x 30 cm (12 in), 2 x 25 cm (10 in), 12 x 10 cm (4 in), or 18 x 8 cm (3 in) turnovers**

## BUTTERMILK DOUGH

**250 g (8 oz) plain (baker's/all-purpose) flour**
**½ teaspoon salt**
**½ teaspoon bicarbonate of soda**
**20 g (½ oz) butter**
**170 ml (6 fl oz) buttermilk**

**1** This step may be done in a processor. Put flour, salt and bicarbonate of soda into a bowl and stir to blend. Rub in butter until evenly dispersed, then gradually stir in buttermilk. When mixture begins to clump together, transfer to a floured surface.

**2** Knead until uniform, spongy and smooth. Cover and set aside to rest at room temperature for 20 minutes before use.

**Makes 1 x 30 cm (12 in), 2 x 25 cm (10 in), 12 x 10 cm (4 in), or 18 x 8 cm (3 in) turnovers**

# AVOCADO, SMOKED MOZZARELLA AND TOMATO CALZONE

**1 x recipe Buttermilk Dough, (see recipe page 84)**

**extra virgin olive oil for brushing**

**125 g (4 oz) grated parmesan cheese**

**125 g (4 oz) shredded smoked mozzarella cheese**

**500 g (16 oz) firm fresh tomatoes, ideally egg or San Marzano**

**1 small red onion, finely sliced**

**2 large slightly under-ripe avocados, peeled, seeded and sliced**

**3 tablespoons chopped fresh basil**

**2 to 3 tablespoons olive oil**

**salt**

**freshly ground black pepper**

**1** Preheat oven to 240°C (465°F) and brush a heavy-duty baking tray with oil.

**2** Roll out dough to a circle of approximately 30 cm (12 in) and transfer to baking tray. Brush lightly with oil.

**3** Distribute cheeses over the surface to within 2 cm (¾ in) of the edge.

**4** Plunge each tomato into boiling water for 5 to 6 seconds, then peel and slice. Arrange on one half of dough along with onion, avocado and basil. Drizzle over 2 to 3 tablespoons olive oil, and season to taste with salt and pepper.

**5** Fold the other half over to cover filling, matching edges. Seal edges by rolling over and pinching together.

**6** Brush surface with olive oil and transfer immediately to oven. Bake until dough is golden, 15 to 20 minutes. Serve at once.

**MAKES 1 X 30 CM (12 IN) CALZONE, ENOUGH FOR 2 AS A MAIN COURSE**

# PRAWN (SHRIMP) AND FENNEL CALZONI

**1 x recipe Buttermilk Dough, (see recipe page 84)**

**40 g (1½ oz) butter**

**200 g (6½ oz) thinly sliced fennel bulb**

**1½ tablespoons flour**

**150 ml (5 fl oz) cream**

**salt and white pepper to taste**

**200 g (6½ oz) peeled cooked prawns (if large, cut into pieces)**

**1 egg, beaten with 1 tablespoon water**

**1** Preheat oven to 230°C (450°F) and brush a heavy-duty baking tray with oil.

**2** Divide dough in half and roll each out on a floured surface to rounds approximately 25 cm (10 in) across; rest 10 minutes.

**3** Melt butter in a saucepan and gently soften fennel, stirring often for 10 minutes. Do not brown. Stir in flour, then add cream and salt and pepper. Cook over a low heat, stirring often, until a very thick sauce forms. Remove from heat and cool for 5 minutes before mixing in prawns.

**4** Divide filling between the two circles of dough, placing it in the middle and leaving a 4 cm (1½ in) rim. Brush rims with beaten egg. Working on one at a time, fold dough over filling so that outer edges match up. Press to seal, trim, and seal again with the tines of a fork or by hand. Transfer to prepared tray and brush surface with beaten egg. Rest for 10 minutes.

**5** Transfer to oven and bake 10 minutes. Reduce temperature to 200°C (400°F) and bake until golden, approximately 20 minutes more. Serve at once.

**MAKES 2 X 25 CM (10 IN) CALZONI, A MAIN MEAL FOR 2**

**≈ AVOCADO, SMOKED MOZZARELLA AND TOMATO CALZONE**

*Calzone, really a pizza which has been folded over, requires a very high heat. A strong, heavy-duty baking tray is desirable to avoid buckling at these temperatures, and one with a slight rim will catch any leakage of the filling.*

*Cooking avocado can often affect its taste. Here, encased in pastry, it retains its texture and flavour, provided that the fruit is slightly under-ripe.*

**≈ PRAWN (SHRIMP) AND FENNEL CALZONI**

*'Calzone' (singular) is old Naples slang for trousers or breeches, and the plump, smooth dough of a baked calzone does look a little like buttoned breeches on sturdy thighs. The original calzoni were sausages or salami encased in dough, so perhaps that makes the image clearer!*

**≈ Smoked Salmon and Leek Panzarotti**

*'Panzarotti' is another word from Naples dialect and it is used to describe small parcels of filled pizza dough. Like calzoni they originated in another Italian region but the Neapolitans adapted them to their ever-present pizza dough. And the literal translation? Stomach — supposedly because when baked or fried they puff up and distend.*

# SMOKED SALMON AND LEEK PANZAROTTI

**1 x recipe Olive Oil and White Wine Dough, (see recipe page 84)**

**40 g (1½ oz) butter**

**200 g (6½ oz) finely sliced leeks, white part only**

**1½ tablespoons flour**

**150 ml (5 fl oz) milk**

**a pinch each nutmeg and white pepper**

**150 g (5 oz) thickly sliced smoked salmon, cut into 1.5 cm (¾ in) strips**

**½ teaspoon chopped dill**

**1 egg beaten with 1 to 2 tablespoons water**

**1** Preheat oven to 220°C (425°F) and lightly brush two baking trays with oil.

**2** Divide dough in half and roll each piece out on a lightly floured surface to a 3 mm (⅛ in) thickness. Using a cookie cutter or an upturned glass, cut out eighteen 8 cm (3 in) circles. (The scraps from the first roll can be re-rolled once.) Rest, covered, for 10 minutes before proceeding.

**3** In the meantime, melt butter in a saucepan and add leeks. Cook over a gentle heat until softened but not brown, 5 minutes. Stir in flour, then gradually add milk. Cook, stirring, until thickened. Season with nutmeg and pepper, then set aside to cool 5 minutes before stirring through smoked salmon and dill.

**4** Working a few at a time, brush dough with egg mix then place a teaspoon of filling in the centre. Fold one side of dough over filling to meet the other side, matching the edges up. Press to seal, trim, then press together once more with the tines of a fork. Brush surfaces with egg mixture. Transfer to prepared trays and bake until golden, about 15 minutes.

**Makes 18 panzarotti**

# FLAT RICOTTA TURNOVER

**1 x recipe Buttermilk Dough, (see recipe page 84)**

**300 g (10 oz) ricotta cheese**

**125 g (4 oz) grated mozzarella cheese**

**3 tablespoons grated parmesan cheese**

**80 g (2½ oz) salami, diced**

**60 g (2 oz) prosciutto, cut into small pieces**

**2 tablespoons finely chopped parsley**

**salt and freshly ground black pepper**

**2 eggs, lightly beaten**

**1 tablespoon olive oil**

**2 tablespoons grated romano (or parmesan) cheese**

**1** Preheat oven to 220°C (425°F) and brush a pizza or baking tray with oil.

**2** Roll out and shape dough to a circle of 28 cm to 30 cm (11 in x 12 in) then transfer to prepared tray.

**3** Combine ricotta, mozzarella, parmesan, salami, prosciutto and parsley in a bowl. Season with salt and pepper. Stir in three quarters of beaten eggs, then beat the remainder with olive oil to use for glazing.

**4** Brush around edge of dough with egg/oil mixture. Place filling in the centre of one half of dough then fold the other side over, encasing filling. Press edges together to seal and press down on top of turnover to give a flat half moon shape. Twist edges up and over themselves, then pinch to form a pattern and to further seal in filling. Brush surface with remaining egg/oil mixture, sprinkle romano on top and transfer to oven. Bake for 20 to 25 minutes, or until the dough is golden. Serve immediately, cut into wedges.

**Makes one 30 cm (12 in) turnover**

# SPINACH AND CHEESE PUFFS

**1 x recipe Olive Oil and White Wine Dough, (see recipe page 84)**

**375 g (12 oz) frozen chopped spinach, thawed**

**100 g (3½ oz) cottage cheese, pushed through a sieve**

**salt and pepper**

**1 egg, lightly beaten**

**vegetable oil for frying**

Divide dough in half and roll out each iece on a lightly floured surface to a 3 mm ⅛ in) thickness. Using a cookie cutter or an pturned glass, cut out 12 circles of 10 cm 4 in) diameter. (The scraps from the first oll can be re-rolled once more.) Save some craps for testing the oil later. Roll each circle nce from one side to the other to form an val. Set aside, covered, while making filling.

Wring spinach out well in a tea towel. Put a bowl and mix in cottage cheese. Add salt d pepper to taste, then stir through egg.

**3** Working a few at a time, brush dough ovals with water then place a heaped teaspoon of filling in the centre. Fold over one of the long ends to meet its opposite, enclosing the filling. Press to seal. Using a floured sharp knife, trim cut edges to a point to form a triangle. With gentle pressure the filling can be manoeuvred to match the shape. Set aside on a plate, then refrigerate for 30 minutes before proceeding.

**4** Fill a deep-sided frying pan with oil to approximately 1.5 cm (¾ in) deep and bring to a moderately hot temperature. When oil begins to shimmer toss in a piece of reserved dough to test. It should bubble and start to brown after 8 to 10 seconds.

**5** Working a few at a time begin frying puffs on both sides until golden. It's normal for the dough to blister, but the oil is too hot if the blisters burn and crack. Remove with tongs or a slotted spoon and drain on wire racks set over kitchen paper.

**MAKES 12 PUFFS**

*Spinach and Cheese Puffs*

**≈ SPINACH AND CHEESE PUFFS**

*Reminiscent of the Greek tiropitakia, these little fried breads transport well so are good to take on a picnic.*

*To refresh them if they have been refrigerated, loosely cover with a sheet of foil and place in a hot oven for 5 minutes.*

**≈ Moroccan Spicy Breads**

*Don't be put off by the presence of suet in this recipe. Although it's part of the filling, it also becomes the medium for frying these spicy parcels; it is the same as using oil or butter, but with more flavour.*

# MOROCCAN SPICY BREADS

**1 x recipe Olive Oil and White Wine Dough, (see recipe page 84)**

**3 tablespoons finely chopped parsley**

**1 tablespoon finely chopped mint**

**150 g (5 oz) onion, finely chopped**

**½ teaspoon ground cumin**

**pinch ground cardamom**

**pinch powdered saffron**

**1 teaspoon paprika**

**¼ teaspoon cayenne pepper**

**150 g (5 oz) beef suet, finely chopped (available from butcher shops)**

**1** Divide dough into 6 equal parts. Roll or shape each into a rectangle approximately 20 cm x 34 cm (8 in x 13½ in).

**2** Combine all other ingredients in a blender or food processor to give a coarsely textured paste, or pound with a mortar and pestle.

**3** Divide filling into 6, then, working one at a time, spread filling along the centre third of each dough rectangle. Fold the left side over to cover filling, then the right side over to cover the left side. You will have a rectangle one third the size of the original. Press to flatten, then roll or shape to original size. Repeat folding, but this time fold the right side over centre third, then the left side over the right. Lightly press open edges together, then set aside to rest for 10 minutes.

**4** Heat a griddle or iron frying pan to a moderate heat.

**5** With a fork prick breads 8 to 10 times on each side. Begin frying them, one or two at a time, for approximately 6 minutes on each side or until they are golden and crisp. As they heat the suet will melt and provide the fat for the breads to fry in. Delicious hot or at room temperature.

**Makes 6 breads 12 cm x 20 cm (5 in x 8 in)**

# SPINACH, ZUCCHINI (COURGETTE) AND ONION BREAD

**1 x recipe Buttermilk Dough, (see recipe page 84)**

**100 g (3½ oz) grated zucchini (courgette)**

**salt**

**2 tablespoons olive oil**

**1 red onion, sliced**

**1 garlic clove, minced**

**1 tablespoon sultanas**

**500 g (16 oz) spinach, stalks removed and leaves rinsed and shredded**

**4 tablespoons grated mozzarella cheese**

**salt and freshly ground black pepper**

**olive oil for brushing**

**1** Divide dough in half and roll both out to a circle of 25 cm (10 in) diameter. Cover and set aside to rest.

**2** Sprinkle zucchini with salt and place in a colander to drain for 10 minutes. Squeeze off excess liquid.

**3** Heat oil in a large pan and gently sauté onion until soft, 8 to 10 minutes. Add garlic and sultanas and sauté a further 2 to 3 minutes. Add zucchini, sauté 15 to 20 seconds, then add spinach. Cook over a moderate to high heat until spinach wilts. Remove from heat, allow to cool then stir in mozzarella. Season with salt and pepper.

**4** In the meantime, preheat oven to 200°C (400°F) and brush a baking tray with oil.

**5** Place one circle of dough on prepared tray and brush with olive oil. Spoon filling over its centre, leaving 2 cm (¾ in) free around the edges. Cover with second circle of dough, pressing down around the edges. Twist and pinch edges to seal. Brush with olive oil and rest for 10 minutes before baking. Bake until golden brown, about 20 minutes. Serve warm or cold.

**Makes 1 bread of approximately 23 cm (9 in) diameter**

# CALCIONI

**1 x recipe Olive Oil and White Wine Dough, (see recipe page 84)**

**1 egg yolk, beaten with 1 tablespoon milk**

**1 large tomato, skinned and seeded, then finely chopped (or 9 teaspoons coarse tomato sauce)**

**60 g (2 oz) mozzarella cheese, cut into small dice**

**80 g (2½ oz) mortadella with peppercorns, cut into small dice**

**9 stuffed green olives, halved**

**½ teaspoon dried marjoram, or 1 teaspoon finely chopped fresh**

**paprika or cayenne pepper**

**1** Preheat oven to 200°C (400°F) and brush a baking tray with oil.

**2** Roll out dough on a floured surface to a thickness of 3 mm (⅛ in). With an 8 cm (3 in) cookie cutter cut out 18 circles (the scraps may be re-rolled once). Put 9 aside, covered.

**3** Brush around outer edges of remaining 9 circles with egg/milk mix. Place 1 teaspoon of tomato in the centre of each, followed by some mozzarella and some mortadella cubes, 2 olive halves and a sprinkling of marjoram. Cover with the reserved dough circles, pressing firmly around the edges to seal. Crimp edges with the fingers, or impress with the tines of a fork.

**4** Transfer to prepared tray, brush tops with egg/milk and sprinkle a little paprika over this. Bake until golden brown, 15 to 20 minutes. Serve hot from the oven.

**MAKES NINE 8 CM (3 IN) PASTIES**

# PITTA CALABRESE

**3 tablespoons olive oil**

**20 g (½ oz) butter**

**1 garlic clove, minced**

**750 g (24 oz) onions, thinly sliced**

**250 g (8 oz) fennel bulb, thinly sliced**

**1 teaspoon chopped fresh marjoram or oregano**

**salt and freshly ground black pepper**

**2 x recipe Buttermilk Dough, (see recipe page 84)**

**100 g (3½) provolone or emmenthal cheese, thinly sliced**

**2 tablespoons grated pecorino cheese**

**extra olive oil for brushing**

**1** Heat olive oil and butter in a large frying pan and add garlic, onions, fennel and marjoram. Cook over a low heat, stirring often, until onions are soft, 20 to 25 minutes. Season with salt and pepper.

**2** In the meantime preheat oven to 220°C (425°F). Brush a large baking tray with oil and dust lightly with flour.

**3** Divide dough in two, with one piece a little larger than the other. Roll both out on a floured surface, the first to a circle of 36 cm (14½ in) and the second, 31 cm (12½ in). Transfer the larger to prepared tray.

**4** Spread onion mixture over dough to within 2 cm (¾ in) of the rim. Cover with cheese slices then sprinkle with pecorino. Place second sheet of dough over the onions. Fold bottom rim up and over, press firmly, then impress the outer edge with the tines of a fork. Make impressions over bread surface with the fork, and brush lightly with olive oil. Bake until golden, 25 to 30 minutes. Serve warm.

**MAKES ONE 32 CM (12¾ IN) ROUND BREAD**

**≈ PITTA CALABRESE**

*This ancient dish from Calabria (where pitta means pie) dates back to the time when southern Italy had a strong Arab influence after the Saracen invasion.*

*Panzarotti with Artichokes*

# PANZAROTTI WITH ARTICHOKES

**1 x recipe Olive Oil and White Wine Dough, (see recipe page 84)**

**1 egg, beaten**

**2 tablespoons olive oil**

**20 g (½ oz) butter**

**100 g (3½ oz) lean bacon or pancetta, diced**

**1 small red onion, sliced**

**2 garlic cloves, minced**

**2 tablespoons finely chopped parsley**

**3 artichoke hearts, cut into quarters lengthwise**

**100 g (3½ oz) smoked mozzarella or other naturally smoked cheese, diced**

**salt and freshly ground black pepper**

**oil for frying**

**1** Roll dough out on a floured surface to a 3 mm (⅛ in) thickness. Rest for 10 minutes, then cut out twelve 10 cm (4 in) circles (the dough scraps may be re-rolled once). Brush around the edges with beaten egg.

**2** In the meantime, heat oil and butter in a frying pan then add bacon, onion and garlic. Sauté gently for 10 minutes, adding parsley for the last 1 to 2 minutes. If any liquid remains, increase heat and cook, stirring, until evaporated. Remove from heat.

**3** Place 1 teaspoon bacon/onion mix in the centre of each circle of dough. Add an artichoke heart quarter, some cheese, and salt and pepper to taste. Fold one side of dough over to meet the other, encasing the filling. Press firmly to seal, then impress edges with the tines of a fork. Place on a large plate or oven tray and refrigerate, 30 minutes.

**4** Put oil in a frying pan to a depth of 2 cm (¾ in) and heat. When it begins to shimmer, drop in a small piece of dough. This will dance on the surface when the oil is hot enough. Fry panzarotti, 2 to 3 at a time, until puffed and golden on both sides. Remove with a slotted spoon and drain on absorbent paper before serving.

**MAKES TWELVE 9 CM (3½ IN) PANZAROTTI**

# TUNA CALZONE WITH CAPERS, LIMES AND SHALLOTS

*Any seafood can replace the tuna in this recipe.*

**2 x recipe Buttermilk Dough, (see recipe page 84)**

**2 tablespoons olive oil**

**20 g (½ oz) butter**

**3 green shallots (green onions), finely chopped**

**2 x 440 g (14 oz) tins tuna in brine, drained and broken up**

**salt and freshly ground black pepper**

**3 to 4 tablespoons thick cream**

**1 teaspoon tiny capers**

**1 tablespoon finely chopped parsley**

**½ teaspoon finely grated lime zest**

**olive oil, for brushing**

**1** Preheat oven to 220°C (425°F) and brush a baking tray with oil.

**2** Divide dough into 6 equal parts and roll each out on a floured surface to a circle 4 mm to 5 mm (¼ in) thick. Set aside, covered.

**3** Heat oil and butter in a pan and gently sauté shallots until softened. Remove from heat, add tuna, salt and pepper to taste and stir in just enough cream to unite mixture. Toss through capers, parsley and lime zest.

**4** Divide mixture into 6 parts and place in the centre of dough circles. Draw up sides of each one so that they meet along the top. Press together and crimp a pattern as you seal the seam. Transfer to prepared tray, brush surfaces with olive oil and place in the oven. Bake for 10 minutes, reduce temperature to 190°C (375°F), and bake a further 12 to 15 minutes, or until golden.

**MAKES 6 CALZONI**

# TORTA RUSTICA

**1 x recipe Buttermilk Dough, (see recipe page 84)**

**1 tablespoon olive oil**

**20 g (½ oz) butter**

**1 small onion, thinly sliced**

**½ small green capsicum (pepper), chopped**

**225 g (7 oz) cooked tuna meat (tinned is fine), broken up into pieces**

**2 tablespoons seeded and sliced black olives**

**salt and freshly ground black pepper**

**good pinch chopped oregano, fresh or dried**

**125 g (4 oz) shredded emmenthal or cheddar cheese**

**1 egg, lightly beaten**

**1** Preheat oven to 190°C (375°F) and brush a 23 cm (9 in) cake tin with oil.

**2** Divide dough into two pieces, one slightly larger than the other. On a floured surface roll the larger one out to a 27 cm (10¾ in) circle and line prepared tin with it. Roll out remaining dough to a 24 cm (9½ in) square. Cover both doughs with tea towels and set aside.

**3** Heat olive oil and butter in a pan and gently sauté onion for 8 to 10 minutes. Add green capsicum (pepper) and sauté a further 8 to 10 minutes without browning. Remove from heat and stir in tuna and olives. Season with salt and pepper and toss in oregano. Spoon filling into base and sprinkle cheese over the top.

**4** Cut dough square into 2 cm (¾ in) strips. Attach half, side by side, to the dough on

**≈ TORTA RUSTICA**

*The plaited top for this bread requires a certain amount of dexterity and patience, so if it all gets beyond you, a plain flat dough with several deep slashes is quite acceptable (but not half as attractive!)*

**≈ Empanadas**

*Empanadas are found all over Spain. Small or giant-sized, they are characterised by a very thin dough and a filling of contrasting flavours, often with many ingredients. What they are filled with is always a good representation of the local produce and this recipe, using both fish and sausage, is typical of the coastal province of Galicia.*

**≈ Syrian Lamb Pies**

*There are many variations of sfeeha, small breads with a spicy minced lamb filling. Some are open, looking like little pizzas, while others resemble parcels with the filling encased by dough.*

*Try forming different shapes and varying the sizes, then serving them all together. They are traditionally served hot as an appetiser, accompanied by yoghurt, but they also make great lunch time snacks and the closed ones are good to take on a picnic.*

one side of loaf, and the other half at right angles on an adjoining side. The secret is to have the strips flapping away from and not over the filling. Weave strips in a lattice pattern, always folding the loose ends back away from the direction you're working in. Once you've reached the opposite side, trim and tuck ends around the filling, and straighten up lattice. Brush top with egg then transfer to oven. Bake until golden, 35 to 40 minutes. Serve straight from the oven.

**Serves 6 to 8**

## EMPANADAS

**2 x recipe Olive Oil and White Wine Dough, (see recipe page 84)**

**220 g (7 oz) smoked haddock or other smoked firm-fleshed fish**

**approximately 250 ml (8 fl oz) milk**

**4 tablespoons olive oil**

**1 medium onion, finely chopped**

**1 garlic clove, minced**

**1 medium green capsicum (pepper), cleaned and chopped**

**1 tablespoon flour**

**220 g (7 oz) chorizo sausage or similar, cut into 1 cm (½ in) cubes**

**salt and cayenne pepper**

**oil for frying**

**1** Divide dough in half and roll each out on a floured surface to a very thin sheet 3 mm (⅛ in) thick. Cut out 6 circles of 15 cm (6 in) diameter (the dough scraps can be re-rolled once) and set aside, covered, to rest while filling is being made.

**2** Put fish in a flat flame-proof pan, cover with milk and gently poach until just tender. Remove from pan and cut into 1 cm (½ in) cubes. Strain milk and reserve.

**3** Heat oil in a frying pan and gently sauté onion for 8 to 10 minutes. Add garlic and green capsicum (pepper) and cook, stirring often for another 8 to 10 minutes. Stir in flour, cook 20 to 30 seconds, then add enough of the reserved milk to give a fairly thick sauce. Stir in cooked fish and chorizos, then salt and pepper to taste.

**4** Place a heaped tablespoon of filling in the centre of each circle of dough. Brush around the rims with water, then fold one side over the other to encase filling. Press tightly to seal. As empanadas are filled, put them on a plate and refrigerate until oil is ready.

**5** Put oil in a deep-sided frying pan to a depth of at least 3 cm (1¼ in). Heat until a slight haze shimmers above it, then drop in a small scrap of dough. If it dances on the surface, the oil is ready. Fry empanadas, one or two at a time, until crisp and golden on both sides. Remove with a slotted spoon and drain on paper towels. Serve at once.

**Makes 6 empanadas**

## SYRIAN LAMB PIES

**1 x recipe Buttermilk Dough, (see recipe page 84)**

**3 tablespoons olive oil**

**3 tablespoons pine nuts**

**1 large onion, finely chopped**

**2 garlic cloves, minced**

**½ small green capsicum (pepper), finely chopped**

**650 g (22 oz) minced lamb**

**½ teaspoon cayenne pepper**

**¼ teaspoon ground cumin**

**½ teaspoon allspice**

**salt and freshly ground black pepper**

**1 large tomato (or 3 peeled tinned tomatoes), skinned, seeded and finely chopped**

**2 tablespoons lemon juice**

**1 tablespoon red wine vinegar**

**3 tablespoons finely chopped parsley**

**1** Divide dough into 10 equal portions and roll each out on a floured surface to a diameter of 10 cm (4 in). Rest, covered, for 30 minutes.

2 Heat oil in a frying pan and lightly toast pine nuts. Remove with a slotted spoon and reserve. Add onion to pan and gently sauté until softened, about 8 minutes. Add garlic and green capsicum (pepper), sauté for 2 to 3 minutes, then stir in lamb. Cook, stirring often, until lamb is browned, 5 minutes. Stir in cayenne, cumin and allspice, and season with salt and pepper. Add tomato, lemon juice, vinegar and parsley, increase heat and cook, stirring, for 10 to 15 seconds. Remove from heat, stir in pine nuts and cool for 5 minutes.

3 Preheat oven to 240°C (465°F) and brush 2 heavy-duty baking trays with oil.

4 Divide mixture evenly between dough bases, spooning it onto centre of each circle. On 5 of them, bring up opposite sides of dough to meet over filling. Pinch edges together to form a spine, leaving the ends slightly opened. With the remaining 5 circles of dough, bring up 3 equidistant points from the sides to meet on top of the filling. Pinch seams together, leaving an opening in the centre top. Transfer to prepared trays and rest for 10 minutes.

Place one tray above the other in the oven and bake for 5 minutes. Switch trays around and bake a further 5 minutes before reducing heat to 200°C (400°F). Continue baking until golden, 5 to 10 minutes more.

**MAKES 10 PIES**

# PANZAROTTI WITH CHICKEN, SMOKED MOZZARELLA AND PECANS

**1 x recipe Olive Oil and White Wine Dough, (see recipe page 84)**

**250 g (8 oz) cooked chicken meat, cut into small cubes**

**200 g (6½ oz) smoked mozzarella cheese, cut into small cubes**

**1 teaspoon finely chopped fresh mint**

**6 shelled pecan halves, coarsely chopped**

**salt and freshly ground black pepper**

**1 egg, lightly beaten**

1 Preheat oven to 200°C (400°F) and grease a baking tray.

2 Divide dough in half and roll each out on a floured surface to a thickness of 3 mm (⅛ in). Cut out 12 circles of 10 cm (4 in) diameter. (The dough scraps may be re-rolled once.)

3 Combine chicken, smoked mozzarella, mint and pecans, and season to taste with salt and pepper. Unite with half the beaten egg.

4 Brush around the rims of dough circles with beaten egg. Place a heaped teaspoon of filling in the centre of each circle. Fold one side of dough over filling to meet its opposite, forming a half moon shape. Press edges together tightly and trim. Transfer to prepared tray and rest for 10 minutes.

5 Brush tops with remaining egg, transfer tray to oven and bake until golden, 15 to 20 minutes. Best served warm.

**MAKES 12 PANZAROTTI**

**≈ PANZAROTTI WITH CHICKEN, SMOKED MOZZARELLA AND PECANS**

*A variation on this combination is to use smoked chicken or turkey with bocconcini.*

**≈ CHIZZE**

*Resembling giant ravioli, these deep-fried pizza squares are perfect for a snack or to serve as an entrée with a light tomato sauce.*

# CHIZZE

**1 recipe Olive Oil and White Wine Dough, (see recipe page 84)**

**50 g (2 oz) cooked, well-drained spinach**

**50 g (2 oz) ricotta cheese**

**75 g (2½ oz) grated parmesan cheese**

**1 teaspoon chopped toasted pistachio kernels**

**salt and freshly ground black pepper**

**1 egg white, lightly beaten**

**oil for deep-frying**

**1** Roll out dough on a floured surface to a rectangle 15 cm x 35 cm (6 in x 14 in). Cut into 5 cm (2 in) squares with a zigzag pastry cutter.

**2** Finely chop spinach then combine with ricotta, parmesan and pistachios. Season to taste with salt and pepper.

**3** Brush around edges of half the dough squares with egg white. Place a teaspoon of spinach mixture in the centre, then cover with the remaining squares of dough. Press to seal edges, and neaten them with the pastry wheel if necessary. Place in a single layer on a tray and refrigerate while oil is heating.

**4** Heat oil in a deep-fryer, or in a saucepan at a depth of at least 5 cm (2 in). It is hot enough when a small piece of dough dances on the surface. Deep-fry squares, a few at a time, until golden on both sides. Drain on absorbent paper and serve at once.

**MAKES 21 SQUARES**

# EGG AND PROSCIUTTO BREAD

**1½ x recipe Buttermilk Dough, (see recipe page 84)**

**200 g (6½ oz) lean prosciutto**

**6 eggs (5 whole, 1 separated)**

**freshly ground black pepper**

**1 teaspoon shredded fresh basil**

**white of separated egg beaten with 1 tablespoon milk**

**1** Preheat oven to 190°C (375°F) and grease a shallow-sided ovenproof dish of approximately 18 cm x 28 cm (7 in x 11 in).

**2** Divide dough in half and roll each out to a rectangle 21 cm x 31 cm (8½ in x 12½ in) or (3 cm/1¼ in) larger each way than prepared dish). Use one sheet to line prepared dish, forming 1.5 cm (¾ in) sides. Spread prosciutto in a single layer over the bottom. Break eggs on top and put in egg yolk. Prick any yolks which haven't yet broken so that yolks and whites run into themselves and cover prosciutto. Season with pepper and sprinkle on basil. Brush dough rim with egg/milk mix.

**3** Trim remaining sheet of dough to fit the top of the bread; reserve trimmings. Cover bread with this top layer, matching up sides Fold exposed sides down onto the top layer and press to seal. Work around the rim by hand, crimping and sealing as you go. Brush surface with egg/milk mix and make a few small slashes with the point of a knife. Use dough trimmings to make a lattice pattern for the top. Transfer to oven and bake until golden, approximately 30 minutes.

**SERVES 4 TO 6**

# GLOSSARY

**Balsamic vinegar (aceto balsamico)** – from Modena in northern Italy, made from the boiled down must of selected grapes. Is syrupy and aromatic after being aged in a series of different wood barrels. Use sparingly.

**Bocconcini** – small balls of fresh mozzarella cheese with a limited shelf life.

**Emmenthal cheese (emmenthaler)** – otherwise known as Swiss cheese. Contains large holes, has a slightly nutty taste and melts well.

**Extra virgin olive oil** – made from the cold first pressing of slightly under-ripe olives. The better ones are made without rectifying with chemicals. Has under 1% acidity and like pure olive oil, no cholesterol.

**Fontina cheese** – mild, slightly nutty cheese which melts well.

**Ghee** – clarified butter.

**Mozzarella cheese** – mild, rind-less cheese with good melting qualities. Available fresh (see bocconcini) or matured.

**Olive paste** – pulp of either black or green olives. Also known as olive pâté.

**Pancetta** – unsmoked bacon which has been cured in spices.

**Parmesan cheese** – there are two qualities, grana pedano and parmigiano reggiano. The latter is the best quality and must be aged for at least 2 years before released for sale.

**Parsley** – for all these recipes use the large, flat-leaf variety

**Pecorino cheese** – originally a sheep's milk cheese, is sharper and more piquant than parmesan.

**Polenta** – a grain made from corn (maize), is usually a coarse yellow meal but when finely ground becomes a fine white flour.

**Prosciutto** (parma ham) – uncooked, unsmoked ham which has been salted and air cured.

**Ricotta cheese** – fresh cheese made from the whey of milk.

**Romano cheese** – a style of pecorino cheese.

**Suet** – hard fat from beef or lamb loins, or from around the kidneys. Available from butchers.

**Sun-dried tomatoes (pommodori secchi)** – available marinated in oil, or in the dry state. If dry, they must be reconstituted before use. Also available as a spreadable pulp, known as paste or pâté.

## OVEN TEMPERATURES

| TEMPERATURES | CELSIUS (°C) | FAHRENHEIT (°F) | GAS MARK |
|---|---|---|---|
| Very slow | 120 | 250 | ½ |
| Slow | 150 | 300 | 2 |
| Moderately slow | 160-180 | 320-350 | 3-4 |
| Moderate | 190-200 | 375-400 | 5-6 |
| Moderately hot | 220-230 | 425-450 | 7 |
| Hot | 250-260 | 475-500 | 8-9 |

NOTE: We developed the recipes in this book in Australia where the tablespoon measure is 20 ml. In many other countries the tablespoon is 15 ml. For most recipes this difference will not be noticeable.

However, for recipes using baking powder, gelatine, bicarbonate of soda, small amounts of flour and cornflour, we suggest you add an extra teaspoon for each tablespoon specified.

# Index